MznLnx

Missing Links Exam Preps

Exam Prep for

Intermediate Algebra for College Students

Angel, 6th Edition

The MznLnx Exam Prep is your link from the texbook and lecture to your exams.
The MznLnx Exam Preps are unauthorized and comprehensive reviews of your textbooks.

All material provided by MznLnx and Rico Publications (c) 2010
Textbook publishers and textbook authors do not particpate in or contribute to these reviews.

MznLnx

Rico
Publications

Exam Prep for Intermediate Algebra for College Students
6th Edition
Angel

Publisher: Raymond Houge
Assistant Editor: Michael Rouger
Text and Cover Designer: Lisa Buckner
Marketing Manager: Sara Swagger
Project Manager, Editorial Production: Jerry Emerson
Art Director: Vernon Lowerui

Product Manager: Dave Mason
Editorial Assitant: Rachel Guzmanji
Pedagogy: Debra Long
Cover Image: Jim Reed/Getty Images
Text and Cover Printer: City Printing, Inc.
Compositor: Media Mix, Inc.

(c) 2010 Rico Publications
ALL RIGHTS RESERVED. No part of this work covered by the copyright may be reproduced or used in any form or by an means--graphic, electronic, or mechanical, including photocopying, recording, taping, Web distribution, information storage, and retrieval systems, or in any other manner--without the written permission of the publisher.

For more information about our products, contact us at:
Dave.Mason@RicoPublications.com

For permission to use material from this text or product, submit a request online to:
Dave.Mason@RicoPublications.com

Printed in the United States
ISBN:

Contents

CHAPTER 1
Basic Concepts — 1

CHAPTER 2
Equations and Inequalities — 16

CHAPTER 3
Graphs and Functions — 34

CHAPTER 4
Systems of Equations and Inequalities — 51

CHAPTER 5
Polynomials and Polynomial Functions — 65

CHAPTER 6
Rational Expressions and Equations — 80

CHAPTER 7
Roots, Radicals, and Complex Numbers — 96

CHAPTER 8
Quadratic Functions — 112

CHAPTER 9
Exponential and Logarithmic Functions — 128

CHAPTER 10
Conic Sections — 144

CHAPTER 11
Sequences, Series, and the Binomial Theorem — 149

ANSWER KEY — 154

TO THE STUDENT

COMPREHENSIVE

The *MznLnx* Exam Prep series is designed to help you pass your exams. Editors at MznLnx review your textbooks and then prepare these practice exams to help you master the textbook material. Unlike study guides, workbooks, and practice tests provided by the texbook publisher and textbook authors, *MznLnx* gives you **all** of the material in each chapter in exam form, not just samples, so you can be sure to nail your exam.

MECHANICAL

The MznLnx Exam Prep series creates exams that will help you learn the subject matter as well as test you on your understanding. Each question is designed to help you master the concept. Just working through the exams, you gain an understanding of the subject--its a simple mechanical process that produces success.

INTEGRATED STUDY GUIDE AND REVIEW

MznLnx is not just a set of exams designed to test you, its also a comprehensive review of the subject content. Each exam question is also a review of the concept, making sure that you will get the answer correct without having to go to other sources of material. You learn as you go! Its the easiest way to pass an exam.

HUMOR

Studying can be tedious and dry. MznLnx's instructional design includes moderate humor within the exam questions on occassion, to break the tedium and revitalize the brain

Chapter 1. Basic Concepts

1. In set theory and other branches of mathematics, the _____ of a collection of sets is the set that contains everything that belongs to any of the sets, but nothing else.
   a. Union0
   b. Thing
   c. Undefined
   d. Undefined

2. In mathematics, the _____ of two sets A and B is the set that contains all elements of A that also belong to B (or equivalently, all elements of B that also belong to A), but no other elements.
   a. Intersection0
   b. Thing
   c. Undefined
   d. Undefined

3. In mathematics, a _____ may be described informally as a number that can be given by an infinite decimal representation.
   a. Thing
   b. Real number0
   c. Undefined
   d. Undefined

4. In arithmetic and algebra, when a number or expression is both preceded and followed by a binary operation, an _____ is required for which operation should be applied first.
   a. Thing
   b. Order of operations0
   c. Undefined
   d. Undefined

5. _____ is a mathematical operation, written a^n, involving two numbers, the base a and the exponent n.
   a. Exponentiating0
   b. Thing
   c. Undefined
   d. Undefined

6. _____ is a mathematical operation, written a^n, involving two numbers, the base a and the exponent n.
   a. Thing
   b. Exponentiation0
   c. Undefined
   d. Undefined

7. _____ is a branch of mathematics concerning the study of structure, relation and quantity.
   a. Concept
   b. Algebra0
   c. Undefined
   d. Undefined

8. A _____ is a negotiable instrument instructing a financial institution to pay a specific amount of a specific currency from a specific demand account held in the maker/depositor's name with that institution. Both the maker and payee may be natural persons or legal entities.
   a. Thing
   b. Check0
   c. Undefined
   d. Undefined

9. Acid _____ ratio measures the ability of a company to use its near cash or quick assets to immediately extinguish its current liabilities.
   a. Test0
   b. Thing
   c. Undefined
   d. Undefined

10. _____ is the property of a physical object that quantifies the amount of matter and energy it is equivalent to.
    a. Thing
    b. Mass0
    c. Undefined
    d. Undefined

Chapter 1. Basic Concepts

11. _____ element of an element x with respect to a binary operation * with identity element e is an element y such that x * y = y * x = e. In particular,
    a. Thing
    b. Inverse0
    c. Undefined
    d. Undefined

12. _____ is a set, with some particular properties and usually some additional structure, such as the operations of addition or multiplication, for instance.
    a. Space0
    b. Thing
    c. Undefined
    d. Undefined

13. In business, particularly accounting, a _____ is the time intervals that the accounts, statement, payments, or other calculations cover.
    a. Thing
    b. Period0
    c. Undefined
    d. Undefined

14. A _____ is a deliberate process for transforming one or more inputs into one or more results.
    a. Thing
    b. Calculation0
    c. Undefined
    d. Undefined

15. _____ are a measure of time.
    a. Thing
    b. Minutes0
    c. Undefined
    d. Undefined

16. In geometry, the _____ of an object is a point in some sense in the middle of the object.
    a. Thing
    b. Center0
    c. Undefined
    d. Undefined

17. A _____ is a symbolic representation denoting a quantity or expression. It often represents an "unknown" quantity that has the potential to change.
    a. Thing
    b. Variable0
    c. Undefined
    d. Undefined

18. In mathematics and the mathematical sciences, a _____ is a fixed, but possibly unspecified, value. This is in contrast to a variable, which is not fixed.
    a. Constant0
    b. Thing
    c. Undefined
    d. Undefined

19. In combinatorial mathematics, a _____ is an un-ordered collection of unique elements.
    a. Concept
    b. Combination0
    c. Undefined
    d. Undefined

20. An _____ is a combination of numbers, operators, grouping symbols and/or free variables and bound variables arranged in a meaningful way which can be evaluated..
    a. Expression0
    b. Thing
    c. Undefined
    d. Undefined

Chapter 1. Basic Concepts 3

21. _____ are objects, characters, or other concrete representations of ideas, concepts, or other abstractions.
   a. Thing
   b. Symbols0
   c. Undefined
   d. Undefined

22. An _____ or member of a set is an object that when collected together make up the set.
   a. Element0
   b. Thing
   c. Undefined
   d. Undefined

23. In mathematics, the _____, or members of a set or more generally a class are all those objects which when collected together make up the set or class.
   a. Thing
   b. Elements0
   c. Undefined
   d. Undefined

24. The _____, the average in everyday English, which is also called the arithmetic _____ (and is distinguished from the geometric _____ or harmonic _____). The average is also called the sample _____. The expected value of a random variable, which is also called the population _____.
   a. Thing
   b. Mean0
   c. Undefined
   d. Undefined

25. _____ is the state of being greater than any finite real or natural number, however large.
   a. Infinite0
   b. Thing
   c. Undefined
   d. Undefined

26. In mathematics, a set is called _____ if there is a bijection between the set and some set of the form {1, 2, ..., n} where n is a natural number.
   a. Finite0
   b. Thing
   c. Undefined
   d. Undefined

27. In mathematics, a _____ occurs if there is a bijection between the set and some set of the form 1, 2, ..., n where n is a natural number.
   a. Finite set0
   b. Concept
   c. Undefined
   d. Undefined

28. In mathematics, a _____ can mean either an element of the set {1, 2, 3, ...} (i.e the positive integers or the counting numbers) or an element of the set {0, 1, 2, 3, ...} (i.e. the non-negative integers).
   a. Thing
   b. Natural number0
   c. Undefined
   d. Undefined

29. The _____ are the only integral domain whose positive elements are well-ordered, and in which order is preserved by addition. Like the natural numbers, the _____ form a countably infinite set. The set of all _____ is usually denoted in mathematics by a boldface Z.
   a. Integers0
   b. Thing
   c. Undefined
   d. Undefined

30. In mathematics and more specifically set theory, the _____ set is the unique set which contains no elements.

Chapter 1. Basic Concepts

    a. Empty0
    c. Undefined
    b. Thing
    d. Undefined

31. In measure theory, a _____ is a set that is negligible for the purposes of the measure in question.
    a. Concept
    b. Null set0
    c. Undefined
    d. Undefined

32. Mathematical _____ is used to represent ideas.
    a. Thing
    b. Notation0
    c. Undefined
    d. Undefined

33. In mathematics, an _____ is a statement about the relative size or order of two objects.
    a. Thing
    b. Inequality0
    c. Undefined
    d. Undefined

34. In mathematics, an inequality is a statement about the relative size or order of two objects. For example 14 > 10, or 14 is _____ 10.
    a. Greater than0
    b. Thing
    c. Undefined
    d. Undefined

35. A _____ is a one-dimensional picture in which the integers are shown as specially-marked points evenly spaced on a line.
    a. Thing
    b. Number line0
    c. Undefined
    d. Undefined

36. In common philosophical language, a proposition or _____, is the content of an assertion, that is, it is true-or-false and defined by the meaning of a particular piece of language.
    a. Statement0
    b. Concept
    c. Undefined
    d. Undefined

37. In geometry, an _____ is a point at which a line segment or ray terminates.
    a. Endpoint0
    b. Thing
    c. Undefined
    d. Undefined

38. In Euclidean geometry, a _____ is the set of all points in a plane at a fixed distance, called the radius, from a given point, the center.
    a. Circle0
    b. Thing
    c. Undefined
    d. Undefined

39. In mathematics, _____ geometry was the traditional name for the geometry of three-dimensional Euclidean space — for practical purposes the kind of space we live in.
    a. Thing
    b. Solid0
    c. Undefined
    d. Undefined

40. In mathematics, a _____ number is a number which can be expressed as a ratio of two integers. Non-integer _____ numbers (commonly called fractions) are usually written as the vulgar fraction a / b, where b is not zero.

a. Thing
c. Undefined
b. Rational0
d. Undefined

41. A _____ decimal is a number whose decimal representation eventually becomes periodic (i.e. the same number sequence _____ indefinitely).
   a. Thing
   c. Undefined
   b. Repeating0
   d. Undefined

42. A _____ decimal is a decimal fraction which ends after a definite number of digits.
   a. Thing
   c. Undefined
   b. Terminating0
   d. Undefined

43. The _____ (symbol _____) and the millibar (symbol mbar, also mb) are units of pressure.
   a. Bar0
   c. Undefined
   b. Thing
   d. Undefined

44. In plane geometry, a _____ is a polygon with four equal sides, four right angles, and parallel opposite sides. In algebra, the _____ of a number is that number multiplied by itself.
   a. Thing
   c. Undefined
   b. Square0
   d. Undefined

45. In mathematics, a _____ of a number x is a number r such that $r^2 = x$, or in words, a number r whose square (the result of multiplying the number by itself) is x.
   a. Square root0
   c. Undefined
   b. Thing
   d. Undefined

46. Recurring or _____ are numbers which when expressed as decimals have a set of "final" digits which repeat an infinite number of times.
   a. Thing
   c. Undefined
   b. Repeating decimals0
   d. Undefined

47. In mathematics, a _____ of a complex-valued function f is a member x of the domain of f such that f(x) vanishes at x, that is, $x : f(x) = 0$.
   a. Root0
   c. Undefined
   b. Thing
   d. Undefined

48. In mathematics, an _____ number is any real number that is not a rational number- that is, it is a number which cannot be expressed as a fraction m/n, where m and n are integers.
   a. Thing
   c. Undefined
   b. Irrational0
   d. Undefined

49. In mathematics, an _____ is any real number that is not a rational number ¡ª that is, it is a number which cannot be expressed as m/n, where m and n are integers.
   a. Irrational number0
   c. Undefined
   b. Thing
   d. Undefined

50. In mathematics, _____ are any real number that is not a rational number ¡ª that is, it is a number which cannot be expressed as m/n, where m and n are integers.
   a. Irrational numbers0
   b. Thing
   c. Undefined
   d. Undefined

51. A _____ is a set whose members are members of another set or a set contained within another set.
   a. Thing
   b. Subset0
   c. Undefined
   d. Undefined

52. In mathematics, a _____ can mean either an element of the set {1, 2, 3, ...} (i.e the positive integers) or an element of the set {0, 1, 2, 3, ...} (i.e. the non-negative integers).
   a. Concept
   b. Whole number0
   c. Undefined
   d. Undefined

53. Deductive _____ is the kind of _____ in which the conclusion is necessitated by, or reached from, previously known facts (the premises).
   a. Reasoning0
   b. Thing
   c. Undefined
   d. Undefined

54. In mathematics, a _____ is the result of multiplying, or an expression that identifies factors to be multiplied.
   a. Thing
   b. Product0
   c. Undefined
   d. Undefined

55. _____ is a synonym for information.
   a. Thing
   b. Data0
   c. Undefined
   d. Undefined

56. In mathematics, suppose C is a collection of mathematical objects. Then we say that C is _____ if every c , C is uniquely determined by less information about c than one would expect.
   a. Thing
   b. Rigid0
   c. Undefined
   d. Undefined

57. In mathematics, there are several meanings of _____ depending on the subject.
   a. Thing
   b. Degree0
   c. Undefined
   d. Undefined

58. Mathematical _____ really refers to two distinct areas of research: the first is the application of the techniques of formal _____ to mathematics and mathematical reasoning, and the second, in the other direction, the application of mathematical techniques to the representation and analysis of formal _____.
   a. Thing
   b. Logic0
   c. Undefined
   d. Undefined

59. In computing, a _____ can be defined as a structured collection of records or data that is stored in a computer so that a program can consult it to answer queries.

Chapter 1. Basic Concepts

    a. Database0
    b. Thing
    c. Undefined
    d. Undefined

60. _____ is the mathematical action of repeatedly adding or subtracting one, usually to find out how many objects there are or to set aside a desired number of objects.
    a. Counting0
    b. Thing
    c. Undefined
    d. Undefined

61. A _____ of a number is the product of that number with any integer.
    a. Multiple0
    b. Thing
    c. Undefined
    d. Undefined

62. _____, Inc. commonly known simply as _____, is a major American supplier of athletic shoes, apparel and sports equipment.
    a. Thing
    b. Nike0
    c. Undefined
    d. Undefined

63. _____ (Groups, Algorithms and Programming) is a computer algebra system for computational discrete algebra with particular emphasis on, but not restricted to, computational group theory.
    a. Thing
    b. Gap0
    c. Undefined
    d. Undefined

64. _____ is a mathematical science pertaining to the collection, analysis, interpretation or explanation, and presentation of data. It is applicable to a wide variety of academic disciplines, from the physical and social sciences to the humanities.
    a. Statistics0
    b. Thing
    c. Undefined
    d. Undefined

65. A _____ is an illustration used in the branch of mathematics known as set theory. It shows all of the possible mathematical or logical relationships between sets.
    a. Venn diagram0
    b. Thing
    c. Undefined
    d. Undefined

66. A _____ is a simplified and structured visual representation of concepts, ideas, constructions, relations, statistical data, anatomy etc used in all aspects of human activities to visualize and clarify the topic.
    a. Thing
    b. Diagram0
    c. Undefined
    d. Undefined

67. In mathematics, the _____ (or modulus) of a real number is its numerical value without regard to its sign.
    a. Thing
    b. Absolute value0
    c. Undefined
    d. Undefined

68. In mathematics, the additive inverse, or _____ of a number n is the number that, when added to n, yields zero. The additive inverse of n is denoted −n. For example, 7 is −7, because 7 + (−7) = 0, and the additive inverse of −0.3 is 0.3, because −0.3 + 0.3 = 0.

Chapter 1. Basic Concepts

  a. Opposite0
  b. Thing
  c. Undefined
  d. Undefined

69. In mathematics, the _____ inverse, or opposite, of a number n is the number that, when added to n, yields zero. The _____ inverse of n is denoted −n.
  a. Thing
  b. Additive0
  c. Undefined
  d. Undefined

70. In mathematics, the _____ of a number n is the number that, when added to n, yields zero. The _____ of n is denoted −n. For example, 7 is −7, because 7 + (−7) = 0, and the _____ of −0.3 is 0.3, because −0.3 + 0.3 = 0.
  a. Additive inverse0
  b. Thing
  c. Undefined
  d. Undefined

71. A _____ is a number that is less than zero.
  a. Negative number0
  b. Thing
  c. Undefined
  d. Undefined

72. The _____ of measurement are a globally standardized and modernized form of the metric system.
  a. Thing
  b. Units0
  c. Undefined
  d. Undefined

73. A _____ is the result of the addition of a set of numbers. The numbers may be natural numbers, complex numbers, matrices, or still more complicated objects. An infinite _____ is a subtle procedure known as a series.
  a. Sum0
  b. Thing
  c. Undefined
  d. Undefined

74. A _____ is the part of a fraction that tells how many equal parts make up a whole, and which is used in the name of the fraction: "halves", "thirds", "fourths" or "quarters", "fifths" and so on.
  a. Concept
  b. Denominator0
  c. Undefined
  d. Undefined

75. A _____ signifies a point or points of probability on a subject e.g., the _____ of creativity, which allows for the formation of rule or norm or law by interpretation of the phenomena events that can be created.
  a. Principle0
  b. Thing
  c. Undefined
  d. Undefined

76. In Graph theory, a _____ is a digraph with weighted edges.
  a. Concept
  b. Network0
  c. Undefined
  d. Undefined

77. _____, either of the curved-bracket punctuation marks that together make a set of _____
  a. Parentheses0
  b. Thing
  c. Undefined
  d. Undefined

78. Equivalence is the condition of being _____ or essentially equal.

a. Equivalent0 b. Thing
c. Undefined d. Undefined

79. In mathematics, _____ is an elementary arithmetic operation. When one of the numbers is a whole number, _____ is the repeated sum of the other number.
   a. Multiplication0 b. Thing
   c. Undefined d. Undefined

80. In mathematics, a _____ of an integer n, also called a factor of n, is an integer which evenly divides n without leaving a remainder.
   a. Divisor0 b. Thing
   c. Undefined d. Undefined

81. In abstract algebra, _____ consists of sets with binary operations that satisfy certain axioms.
   a. Grouping0 b. Thing
   c. Undefined d. Undefined

82. The _____ is a property of multiplication or addition where the product or sum remains the same, regardless of whether or not the order of the addends or factors are changed.
   a. Commutative property0 b. Thing
   c. Undefined d. Undefined

83. In mathematics, _____ is a property that a binary operation can have. Within an expression containing two or more of the same associative operators in a row, the order of operations does not matter as long as the sequence of the operands is not changed.
   a. Associativity0 b. Thing
   c. Undefined d. Undefined

84. In mathematics, and in particular in abstract algebra, the _____ is a property of binary operations that generalises the distributive law from elementary algebra.
   a. Thing b. Distributive property0
   c. Undefined d. Undefined

85. The _____ of an algebraic expression is the same equation, but without parentheses.
   a. Expanded form0 b. Thing
   c. Undefined d. Undefined

86. In mathematics, the _____ inverse of a number x, denoted 1/x or x^{-1}, is the number which, when multiplied by x, yields 1. The _____ inverse of x is also called the reciprocal of x.
   a. Multiplicative0 b. Thing
   c. Undefined d. Undefined

87. An _____ is an equality that remains true regardless of the values of any variables that appear within it, to distinguish it from an equality which is true under more particular conditions.

Chapter 1. Basic Concepts

a. Identity0
c. Undefined
b. Thing
d. Undefined

88. _____ is a physical property of a system that underlies the common notions of hot and cold; something that is hotter has the greater _____.
   a. Thing
   c. Undefined
   b. Temperature0
   d. Undefined

89. A _____ is a landform that extends above the surrounding terrain in a limited area. A _____ is generally steeper than a hill, but there is no universally accepted standard definition for the height of a _____ or a hill although a _____ usually has an identifiable summit.
   a. Mountain0
   c. Undefined
   b. Thing
   d. Undefined

90. A _____ is a unit of length, usually used to measure distance, in a number of different systems, including Imperial units, United States customary units and Norwegian/Swedish mil. Its size can vary from system to system, but in each is between 1 and 10 kilometers. In contemporary English contexts _____ refers to either:
   a. Mile0
   c. Undefined
   b. Thing
   d. Undefined

91. In banking and accountancy, the outstanding _____ is the amount of money owned, or due, that remains in a deposit account or a loan account at a given date, after all past remittances, payments and withdrawal have been accounted for.
   a. Thing
   c. Undefined
   b. Balance0
   d. Undefined

92. In mathematics, an _____, mean, or central tendency of a data set refers to a measure of the "middle" or "expected" value of the data set.
   a. Average0
   c. Undefined
   b. Concept
   d. Undefined

93. In mathematics, _____ growth occurs when the growth rate of a function is always proportional to the function's current size.
   a. Exponential0
   c. Undefined
   b. Thing
   d. Undefined

94. _____ has many meanings, most of which simply .
   a. Power0
   c. Undefined
   b. Thing
   d. Undefined

95. In mathematics, a _____ is an ordered list of objects. Like a set, it contains members, also called elements or terms, and the number of terms is called the length of the _____. Unlike a set, order matters, and the exact same elements can appear multiple times at different positions in the _____.
   a. Sequence0
   c. Undefined
   b. Thing
   d. Undefined

Chapter 1. Basic Concepts

96. _____ is the symbol used to indicate the nth root of a number
   a. Radical0
   b. Thing
   c. Undefined
   d. Undefined

97. The _____ is the number or expression underneath the radical sign.
   a. Thing
   b. Radicand0
   c. Undefined
   d. Undefined

98. A _____ decimal is a decimal for which there is no digit to the right of the decimal point, as all digits farther from the right are zero.
   a. Nonterminating0
   b. Thing
   c. Undefined
   d. Undefined

99. The word _____ is used in a variety of ways in mathematics.
   a. Index0
   b. Thing
   c. Undefined
   d. Undefined

100. A _____ is a three-dimensional solid object bounded by six square faces, facets, or sides, with three meeting at each vertex.
   a. Cube0
   b. Thing
   c. Undefined
   d. Undefined

101. A _____ of a number is a number a such that $a^3 = x$.
   a. Thing
   b. Cube root0
   c. Undefined
   d. Undefined

102. An _____ of a number a is a number b such that $b^n=a$.
   a. Nth root0
   b. Thing
   c. Undefined
   d. Undefined

103. In mathematics, factorization (British English: factorisation) or factoring is the decomposition of an object (for example, a number, a polynomial, or a matrix) into a product of other objects, or _____, which when multiplied together give the original.
   a. Factors0
   b. Thing
   c. Undefined
   d. Undefined

104. In mathematics, defined and _____ are used to explain whether or not expressions have meaningful, sensible, and unambiguous values.
   a. Undefined0
   b. Thing
   c. Undefined
   d. Undefined

105. _____ is a state located in the southern and southwestern regions of the United States of America.
   a. Thing
   b. Texas0
   c. Undefined
   d. Undefined

Chapter 1. Basic Concepts

106. In mathematics, a _____ is a constant multiplicative factor of a certain object. The object can be such things as a variable, a vector, a function, etc. For example, the _____ of $9x^2$ is 9.
   a. Thing
   b. Coefficient0
   c. Undefined
   d. Undefined

107. A _____ is a special kind of ratio, indicating a relationship between two measurements with different units, such as miles to gallons or cents to pounds.
   a. Rate0
   b. Thing
   c. Undefined
   d. Undefined

108. _____ is the fee paid on borrowed money.
   a. Interest0
   b. Thing
   c. Undefined
   d. Undefined

109. In economics, supply and _____ describe market relations between prospective sellers and buyers of a good.
   a. Thing
   b. Demand0
   c. Undefined
   d. Undefined

110. An _____ is the fee paid on borrow money.
   a. Interest rate0
   b. Concept
   c. Undefined
   d. Undefined

111. Transport or _____ is the movement of people and goods from one place to another.
   a. Transportation0
   b. Thing
   c. Undefined
   d. Undefined

112. _____ is a kind of property which exists as magnitude or multitude. It is among the basic classes of things along with quality, substance, change, and relation.
   a. Thing
   b. Amount0
   c. Undefined
   d. Undefined

113. In mathematics a _____ is a function which defines a distance between elements of a set.
   a. Thing
   b. Metric0
   c. Undefined
   d. Undefined

114. _____ is a way of expressing a number as a fraction of 100 per cent meaning "per hundred".
   a. Percent0
   b. Thing
   c. Undefined
   d. Undefined

115. In mathematics, a _____ is the end result of a division problem. It can also be expressed as the number of times the divisor divides into the dividend.
   a. Quotient0
   b. Thing
   c. Undefined
   d. Undefined

116. The _____ governs the differentiation of products of differentiable functions.

Chapter 1. Basic Concepts

a. Product rule0
b. Thing
c. Undefined
d. Undefined

117. _____ is the largest positive integer that divides both numbers without remainder.
   a. Common Factor0
   b. Thing
   c. Undefined
   d. Undefined

118. A _____ is a numeral used to indicate a count. The most common use of the word today is to name the part of a fraction that tells the number or count of equal parts.
   a. Numerator0
   b. Thing
   c. Undefined
   d. Undefined

119. In mathematics, the multiplicative inverse of a number x, denoted $1/x$ or x^{-1}, is the number which, when multiplied by x, yields 1. The multiplicative inverse of x is also called the _____ of x.
   a. Thing
   b. Reciprocal0
   c. Undefined
   d. Undefined

120. The _____ is a method of finding the derivative of a function that is the quotient of two other functions for which derivatives exist.
   a. Quotient rule0
   b. Thing
   c. Undefined
   d. Undefined

121. _____ is a notation for writing numbers that is often used by scientists and mathematicians to make it easier to write large and small numbers.
   a. Scientific notation0
   b. Thing
   c. Undefined
   d. Undefined

122. _____ forms part of thinking. Considered the most complex of all intellectual functions, _____ has been defined as higher-order cognitive process that requires the modulation and control of more routine or fundamental skills.
   a. Problem solving0
   b. Thing
   c. Undefined
   d. Undefined

123. In geometry, a _____ (Greek words diairo = divide and metro = measure) of a circle is any straight line segment that passes through the centre and whose endpoints are on the circular boundary, or, in more modern usage, the length of such a line segment. When using the word in the more modern sense, one speaks of the _____ rather than a _____, because all diameters of a circle have the same length. This length is twice the radius. The _____ of a circle is also the longest chord that the circle has.
   a. Diameter0
   b. Thing
   c. Undefined
   d. Undefined

124. The metre (or _____, see spelling differences) is a measure of length. It is the basic unit of length in the metric system and in the International System of Units (SI), used around the world for general and scientific purposes.
   a. Concept
   b. Meter0
   c. Undefined
   d. Undefined

125. The decimal separator is a symbol used to mark the boundary between the integral and the fractional parts of a decimal numeral. Terms implying the symbol used are _____ and decimal comma.
- a. Decimal point0
- b. Concept
- c. Undefined
- d. Undefined

126. _____ finance, in finance, a debt security, issued by Issuer
- a. Bond0
- b. Thing
- c. Undefined
- d. Undefined

127. In sociology and biology a _____ is the collection of people or organisms of a particular species living in a given geographic area or space, usually measured by a census.
- a. Thing
- b. Population0
- c. Undefined
- d. Undefined

128. _____ are the basic objects of study in graph theory. Informally speaking, a graph is a set of objects called points, nodes, or vertices connected by links called lines or edges.
- a. Graphs0
- b. Thing
- c. Undefined
- d. Undefined

129. A circular _____ or circle _____ also known as a pie piece is the portion of a circle enclosed by two radii and an arc.
- a. Thing
- b. Sector0
- c. Undefined
- d. Undefined

130. A _____ is a consumption tax charged at the point of purchase for certain goods and services.
- a. Thing
- b. Sales tax0
- c. Undefined
- d. Undefined

131. The population _____ is the total number of human beings alive on the planet Earth at a given time.
- a. Thing
- b. Of the world0
- c. Undefined
- d. Undefined

132. In economics _____ means before deductions brutto, e.g. _____ domestic or national product, or _____ profit or income
- a. Gross0
- b. Thing
- c. Undefined
- d. Undefined

133. A _____ is a function that assigns a number to subsets of a given set.
- a. Measure0
- b. Thing
- c. Undefined
- d. Undefined

134. _____ is a unit of speed, expressing the number of international miles covered per hour.
- a. Miles per hour0
- b. Thing
- c. Undefined
- d. Undefined

Chapter 1. Basic Concepts

135. In mathematics, a _____ is a demonstration that, assuming certain axioms, some statement is necessarily true.
 a. Proof0
 b. Thing
 c. Undefined
 d. Undefined

136. In _____ algebra, a *-ring is an associative ring with an antilinear, antiautomorphism * : A ¨ A which is an involution.
 a. Star0
 b. Thing
 c. Undefined
 d. Undefined

137. A _____ is a unit of length in the metric system, equal to one thousand metres, the current SI base unit of length
 a. Thing
 b. Kilometer0
 c. Undefined
 d. Undefined

138. The _____ is the total number of human beings alive on the planet Earth at a given time.
 a. Thing
 b. World population0
 c. Undefined
 d. Undefined

139. _____ is mass m per unit volume V.
 a. Density0
 b. Thing
 c. Undefined
 d. Undefined

140. _____ is the transport of people on a trip/journey or the process or time involved in a person or object moving from one location to another.
 a. Thing
 b. Travel0
 c. Undefined
 d. Undefined

141. _____ is electromagnetic radiation with a wavelength that is visible to the eye (visible _____) or, in a technical or scientific context, electromagnetic radiation of any wavelength.
 a. Light0
 b. Thing
 c. Undefined
 d. Undefined

142. A _____ is a type of debt. All material things can be lent but this article focuses exclusively on monetary loans. Like all debt instruments, a _____ entails the redistribution of financial assets over time, between the lender and the borrower.
 a. Loan0
 b. Thing
 c. Undefined
 d. Undefined

Chapter 2. Equations and Inequalities

1. The word _____ comes from the Latin word linearis, which means created by lines.
   a. Thing
   b. Linear0
   c. Undefined
   d. Undefined

2. In mathematics, an _____ is a statement about the relative size or order of two objects.
   a. Inequality0
   b. Thing
   c. Undefined
   d. Undefined

3. In mathematics, the _____ (or modulus) of a real number is its numerical value without regard to its sign.
   a. Thing
   b. Absolute value0
   c. Undefined
   d. Undefined

4. In logic, a _____ consists of a logical incompatibility between two or more propositions.
   a. Thing
   b. Contradictions0
   c. Undefined
   d. Undefined

5. An _____ is an equality that remains true regardless of the values of any variables that appear within it, to distinguish it from an equality which is true under more particular conditions.
   a. Thing
   b. Identity0
   c. Undefined
   d. Undefined

6. The material _____, also known as the material implication or truth functional _____, expresses a property of certain conditionals in logic.
   a. Conditional0
   b. Thing
   c. Undefined
   d. Undefined

7. A _____ is an equation in which each term is either a constant or the product of a constant times the first power of a variable.
   a. Linear equation0
   b. Thing
   c. Undefined
   d. Undefined

8. _____ is a branch of mathematics concerning the study of structure, relation and quantity.
   a. Concept
   b. Algebra0
   c. Undefined
   d. Undefined

9. Two mathematical objects are equal if and only if they are precisely the same in every way. This defines a binary relation, _____, denoted by the sign of _____ "=" in such a way that the statement "x = y" means that x and y are equal.
   a. Equality0
   b. Thing
   c. Undefined
   d. Undefined

10. In mathematics, a _____ may be described informally as a number that can be given by an infinite decimal representation.
    a. Thing
    b. Real number0
    c. Undefined
    d. Undefined

Chapter 2. Equations and Inequalities

11. A _____ is a symbolic representation denoting a quantity or expression. It often represents an "unknown" quantity that has the potential to change.
    a. Variable0
    b. Thing
    c. Undefined
    d. Undefined

12. In mathematics, a _____ is a constant multiplicative factor of a certain object. The object can be such things as a variable, a vector, a function, etc. For example, the _____ of $9x^2$ is 9.
    a. Thing
    b. Coefficient0
    c. Undefined
    d. Undefined

13. An _____ is a combination of numbers, operators, grouping symbols and/or free variables and bound variables arranged in a meaningful way which can be evaluated..
    a. Expression0
    b. Thing
    c. Undefined
    d. Undefined

14. A _____ is a symbol or group of symbols, or a word in a natural language that represents a number.
    a. Numeral0
    b. Thing
    c. Undefined
    d. Undefined

15. The _____, the average in everyday English, which is also called the arithmetic _____ (and is distinguished from the geometric _____ or harmonic _____). The average is also called the sample _____. The expected value of a random variable, which is also called the population _____.
    a. Thing
    b. Mean0
    c. Undefined
    d. Undefined

16. In mathematics and the mathematical sciences, a _____ is a fixed, but possibly unspecified, value. This is in contrast to a variable, which is not fixed.
    a. Constant0
    b. Thing
    c. Undefined
    d. Undefined

17. A _____ is the result of the addition of a set of numbers. The numbers may be natural numbers, complex numbers, matrices, or still more complicated objects. An infinite _____ is a subtle procedure known as a series.
    a. Sum0
    b. Thing
    c. Undefined
    d. Undefined

18. In mathematics, a _____ can mean either an element of the set {1, 2, 3, ...} (i.e the positive integers) or an element of the set {0, 1, 2, 3, ...} (i.e. the non-negative integers).
    a. Whole number0
    b. Concept
    c. Undefined
    d. Undefined

19. _____ is a mathematical operation, written a^n, involving two numbers, the base a and the exponent n.
    a. Exponentiating0
    b. Thing
    c. Undefined
    d. Undefined

20. _____ is a mathematical operation, written a^n, involving two numbers, the base a and the exponent n.

Chapter 2. Equations and Inequalities

    a. Thing
    c. Undefined
    b. Exponentiation0
    d. Undefined

21. In mathematics, there are several meanings of _____ depending on the subject.
    a. Thing
    b. Degree0
    c. Undefined
    d. Undefined

22. The _____ is the sum of the exponents of the variables in the term.
    a. Thing
    b. Degree of a term0
    c. Undefined
    d. Undefined

23. In mathematics, and in particular in abstract algebra, the _____ is a property of binary operations that generalises the distributive law from elementary algebra.
    a. Distributive property0
    b. Thing
    c. Undefined
    d. Undefined

24. In common philosophical language, a proposition or _____, is the content of an assertion, that is, it is true-or-false and defined by the meaning of a particular piece of language.
    a. Concept
    b. Statement0
    c. Undefined
    d. Undefined

25. A _____ is a set of possible values that a variable can take on in order to satisfy a given set of conditions, which may include equations and inequalities.
    a. Thing
    b. Solution set0
    c. Undefined
    d. Undefined

26. Equivalence is the condition of being _____ or essentially equal.
    a. Thing
    b. Equivalent0
    c. Undefined
    d. Undefined

27. A _____ is the sum of the elements of a sequence.
    a. Series0
    b. Thing
    c. Undefined
    d. Undefined

28. In mathematics, _____ is an elementary arithmetic operation. When one of the numbers is a whole number, _____ is the repeated sum of the other number.
    a. Thing
    b. Multiplication0
    c. Undefined
    d. Undefined

29. In combinatorial mathematics, a _____ is an un-ordered collection of unique elements.
    a. Concept
    b. Combination0
    c. Undefined
    d. Undefined

30. A _____ is the part of a fraction that tells how many equal parts make up a whole, and which is used in the name of the fraction: "halves", "thirds", "fourths" or "quarters", "fifths" and so on.

Chapter 2. Equations and Inequalities

- a. Denominator0
- b. Concept
- c. Undefined
- d. Undefined

31. _____, either of the curved-bracket punctuation marks that together make a set of _____
- a. Parentheses0
- b. Thing
- c. Undefined
- d. Undefined

32. _____ is a fixed, but possibly unspecified, value. This is in contrast to a variable, which is not fixed.
- a. Thing
- b. Constant term0
- c. Undefined
- d. Undefined

33. A _____ is a negotiable instrument instructing a financial institution to pay a specific amount of a specific currency from a specific demand account held in the maker/depositor's name with that institution. Both the maker and payee may be natural persons or legal entities.
- a. Check0
- b. Thing
- c. Undefined
- d. Undefined

34. _____ is a set, with some particular properties and usually some additional structure, such as the operations of addition or multiplication, for instance.
- a. Thing
- b. Space0
- c. Undefined
- d. Undefined

35. A _____ of a number is the product of that number with any integer.
- a. Multiple0
- b. Thing
- c. Undefined
- d. Undefined

36. The _____ of two integers is the smallest positive integer that is a multiple of both intergers.
- a. Thing
- b. Least common multiple0
- c. Undefined
- d. Undefined

37. In mathematics and more specifically set theory, the _____ set is the unique set which contains no elements.
- a. Thing
- b. Empty0
- c. Undefined
- d. Undefined

38. In measure theory, a _____ is a set that is negligible for the purposes of the measure in question.
- a. Concept
- b. Null set0
- c. Undefined
- d. Undefined

39. _____ forms part of thinking. Considered the most complex of all intellectual functions, _____ has been defined as higher-order cognitive process that requires the modulation and control of more routine or fundamental skills.
- a. Thing
- b. Problem solving0
- c. Undefined
- d. Undefined

40. _____ are a measure of time.

Chapter 2. Equations and Inequalities

a. Minutes0
b. Thing
c. Undefined
d. Undefined

41. In plane geometry, a _____ is a polygon with four equal sides, four right angles, and parallel opposite sides. In algebra, the _____ of a number is that number multiplied by itself.
   a. Square0
   b. Thing
   c. Undefined
   d. Undefined

42. In sociology and biology a _____ is the collection of people or organisms of a particular species living in a given geographic area or space, usually measured by a census.
   a. Population0
   b. Thing
   c. Undefined
   d. Undefined

43. _____ is mass m per unit volume V.
   a. Density0
   b. Thing
   c. Undefined
   d. Undefined

44. A _____ is a unit of length, usually used to measure distance, in a number of different systems, including Imperial units, United States customary units and Norwegian/Swedish mil. Its size can vary from system to system, but in each is between 1 and 10 kilometers. In contemporary English contexts _____ refers to either:
   a. Mile0
   b. Thing
   c. Undefined
   d. Undefined

45. _____ is a way of expressing a number as a fraction of 100 per cent meaning "per hundred".
   a. Thing
   b. Percent0
   c. Undefined
   d. Undefined

46. _____ or life assurance is a contract between the policy owner and the insurer, where the insurer agrees to pay a sum of money upon the occurrence of the policy owner's death.
   a. Thing
   b. Life insurance0
   c. Undefined
   d. Undefined

47. _____, in law and economics, is a form of risk management primarily used to hedge against the risk of a contingent loss.
   a. Thing
   b. Insurance0
   c. Undefined
   d. Undefined

48. _____ is the income from capital investment paid in a series of regular payments.
   a. Annuity0
   b. Thing
   c. Undefined
   d. Undefined

49. A _____ is a form of collective investment that pools money from many investors and invests their money in stocks, bonds, short-term money market instruments, and/or other securities.
   a. Thing
   b. Mutual fund0
   c. Undefined
   d. Undefined

Chapter 2. Equations and Inequalities

50. _____ are objects, characters, or other concrete representations of ideas, concepts, or other abstractions.
   a. Symbols0
   b. Thing
   c. Undefined
   d. Undefined

51. A _____ is an abstract model that uses mathematical language to describe the behavior of a system. Eykhoff defined a _____ as 'a representation of the essential aspects of an existing system which presents knowledge of that system in usable form'.
   a. Thing
   b. Mathematical model0
   c. Undefined
   d. Undefined

52. In mathematics, _____ are essentially word problems that are designed to use mathematical critical thinking in everyday situations.
   a. Application problems0
   b. Thing
   c. Undefined
   d. Undefined

53. _____ are any documents that aim to streamline particular processes according to a set routine.
   a. Guidelines0
   b. Thing
   c. Undefined
   d. Undefined

54. An _____ in policy debate is part of a speech which is flagged as not responding to the line-by-line arguments on the flow.
   a. Overview0
   b. Thing
   c. Undefined
   d. Undefined

55. A _____ is a deliberate process for transforming one or more inputs into one or more results.
   a. Thing
   b. Calculation0
   c. Undefined
   d. Undefined

56. A _____ is a type of debt. All material things can be lent but this article focuses exclusively on monetary loans. Like all debt instruments, a _____ entails the redistribution of financial assets over time, between the lender and the borrower.
   a. Thing
   b. Loan0
   c. Undefined
   d. Undefined

57. In business, particularly accounting, a _____ is the time intervals that the accounts, statement, payments, or other calculations cover.
   a. Period0
   b. Thing
   c. Undefined
   d. Undefined

58. _____ is the fee paid on borrowed money.
   a. Interest0
   b. Thing
   c. Undefined
   d. Undefined

59. _____ is a kind of property which exists as magnitude or multitude. It is among the basic classes of things along with quality, substance, change, and relation.

Chapter 2. Equations and Inequalities

  a. Amount0
  c. Undefined
  b. Thing
  d. Undefined

60. A _____ is a special kind of ratio, indicating a relationship between two measurements with different units, such as miles to gallons or cents to pounds.
  a. Rate0
  c. Undefined
  b. Thing
  d. Undefined

61. _____ or investing is a term with several closely-related meanings in business management, finance and economics, related to saving or deferring consumption.
  a. Thing
  c. Undefined
  b. Investment0
  d. Undefined

62. An _____ is the fee paid on borrow money.
  a. Interest rate0
  c. Undefined
  b. Concept
  d. Undefined

63. _____ interest refers to the fact that whenever interest is calculated, it is based not only on the original principal, but also on any unpaid interest that has been added to the principal.
  a. Thing
  c. Undefined
  b. Compound0
  d. Undefined

64. _____ refers to the fact that whenever interest is calculated, it is based not only on the original principal, but also on any unpaid interest that has been added to the principal. The more frequently interest is compounded, the faster the balance grows.
  a. Concept
  c. Undefined
  b. Compound interest0
  d. Undefined

65. Initial objects are also called _____, and terminal objects are also called final.
  a. Thing
  c. Undefined
  b. Coterminal0
  d. Undefined

66. A _____ or CD is a time deposit, a financial product commonly offered to consumers by banks, thrift institutions, and credit unions.
  a. Thing
  c. Undefined
  b. Certificate of deposit0
  d. Undefined

67. _____ or arithmetics is the oldest and most elementary branch of mathematics, used by almost everyone, for tasks ranging from simple daily counting to advanced science and business calculations.
  a. Thing
  c. Undefined
  b. Arithmetic0
  d. Undefined

68. A _____ is a number, figure, or indicator that appears below the normal line of type, typically used in a formula, mathematical expression, or description of a chemical compound.

Chapter 2. Equations and Inequalities

a. Thing
b. Subscript0
c. Undefined
d. Undefined

69. _____ finance, in finance, a debt security, issued by Issuer
   a. Bond0
   b. Thing
   c. Undefined
   d. Undefined

70. A _____ is a numeral used to indicate a count. The most common use of the word today is to name the part of a fraction that tells the number or count of equal parts.
   a. Numerator0
   b. Thing
   c. Undefined
   d. Undefined

71. A _____ is a quadrilateral, which is defined as a shape with four sides, which has a pair of parallel sides.
   a. Thing
   b. Trapezoid0
   c. Undefined
   d. Undefined

72. A _____ is a method for fastening or securing linear material such as rope by tying or interweaving. It may consist of a length of one or more segments of rope, string, webbing, twine, strap or even chain interwoven so as to create in the line the ability to bind to itself or to some other object - the "load". Knots have been the subject of interest both for their ancient origins, common use, and the mathematical implications of _____ theory.
   a. Knot0
   b. Thing
   c. Undefined
   d. Undefined

73. A _____ is a function that assigns a number to subsets of a given set.
   a. Thing
   b. Measure0
   c. Undefined
   d. Undefined

74. _____ is a unit of speed, expressing the number of international miles covered per hour.
   a. Miles per hour0
   b. Thing
   c. Undefined
   d. Undefined

75. In set theory and other branches of mathematics, the _____ of a collection of sets is the set that contains everything that belongs to any of the sets, but nothing else.
   a. Thing
   b. Union0
   c. Undefined
   d. Undefined

76. In Euclidean geometry, a _____ is the set of all points in a plane at a fixed distance, called the radius, from a given point, the center.
   a. Thing
   b. Circle0
   c. Undefined
   d. Undefined

77. The _____ of a solid object is the three-dimensional concept of how much space it occupies, often quantified numerically.
   a. Thing
   b. Volume0
   c. Undefined
   d. Undefined

Chapter 2. Equations and Inequalities

78. Regrouping is the act of putting ones into groups of 10. For example, the 1 on the far right of 131 would be denoted _____ if the digit of the number being subtracted is larger than 1, such as 131-99.
    a. By 100
    b. Thing
    c. Undefined
    d. Undefined

79. _____ is the ability to hold, receive or absorb, or a measure thereof, similar to the concept of volume.
    a. Capacity0
    b. Concept
    c. Undefined
    d. Undefined

80. A _____ are accounts maintained by commercial banks, savings and loan associations, credit unions, and mutual savings banks that pay interest but can not be used directly as money by, for example, writing a cheque.
    a. Thing
    b. Savings account0
    c. Undefined
    d. Undefined

81. The plus and _____ signs are mathematical symbols used to represent the notions of positive and negative as well as the operations of addition and subtraction.
    a. Thing
    b. Minus0
    c. Undefined
    d. Undefined

82. The word _____ is used in a variety of ways in mathematics.
    a. Thing
    b. Index0
    c. Undefined
    d. Undefined

83. _____ is the property of a physical object that quantifies the amount of matter and energy it is equivalent to.
    a. Mass0
    b. Thing
    c. Undefined
    d. Undefined

84. _____ is a statistical measure of the weight of a person scaled according to height. It was invented between 1830 and 1850 by the Belgian polymath Adolphe Quetelet during the course of developing "social physics".
    a. Body mass index0
    b. Thing
    c. Undefined
    d. Undefined

85. The _____ or kilogramme is the SI base unit of mass. It is defined as being equal to the mass of the international prototype of the _____.
    a. Kilogram0
    b. Thing
    c. Undefined
    d. Undefined

86. _____ is the estimation of a physical quantity such as distance, energy, temperature, or time.
    a. Measurement0
    b. Thing
    c. Undefined
    d. Undefined

87. The metre (or _____, see spelling differences) is a measure of length. It is the basic unit of length in the metric system and in the International System of Units (SI), used around the world for general and scientific purposes.
    a. Concept
    b. Meter0
    c. Undefined
    d. Undefined

Chapter 2. Equations and Inequalities

88. In mathematics a _____ is a function which defines a distance between elements of a set.
  a. Thing
  b. Metric0
  c. Undefined
  d. Undefined

89. The payment of _____ as remuneration for services rendered or products sold is a common way to reward sales people.
  a. Commission0
  b. Thing
  c. Undefined
  d. Undefined

90. Deductive _____ is the kind of _____ in which the conclusion is necessitated by, or reached from, previously known facts (the premises).
  a. Reasoning0
  b. Thing
  c. Undefined
  d. Undefined

91. The _____ of measurement are a globally standardized and modernized form of the metric system.
  a. Thing
  b. Units0
  c. Undefined
  d. Undefined

92. In geometry, a _____ is defined as a quadrilateral where all four of its angles are right angles.
  a. Rectangle0
  b. Thing
  c. Undefined
  d. Undefined

93. In mathematics, a _____ is the result of multiplying, or an expression that identifies factors to be multiplied.
  a. Thing
  b. Product0
  c. Undefined
  d. Undefined

94. The _____ are the only integral domain whose positive elements are well-ordered, and in which order is preserved by addition. Like the natural numbers, the _____ form a countably infinite set. The set of all _____ is usually denoted in mathematics by a boldface Z .
  a. Integers0
  b. Thing
  c. Undefined
  d. Undefined

95. _____ means in succession or back-to-back
  a. Thing
  b. Consecutive0
  c. Undefined
  d. Undefined

96. In geometry, the _____ of an object is a point in some sense in the middle of the object.
  a. Thing
  b. Center0
  c. Undefined
  d. Undefined

97. _____ is the level of functional and/or metabolic efficiency of an organism at both the micro level.
  a. Thing
  b. Health0
  c. Undefined
  d. Undefined

98. In Euclidean geometry, an _____ is a closed segment of a differentiable curve in the two-dimensional plane; for example, a circular _____ is a segment of a circle.

Chapter 2. Equations and Inequalities

a. Concept
b. Arc0
c. Undefined
d. Undefined

99. _____ is the largest city in the state of Texas and the fourth-largest in the United States. As of the 2005 U.S. Census estimate, it had a population of more than 2 million.
   a. Thing
   b. Houston0
   c. Undefined
   d. Undefined

100. The _____ rule, also known as a slipstick, is a mechanical analog computer, consisting of at least two finely divided scales, most often a fixed outer pair and a movable inner one, with a sliding window called the cursor.
   a. Thing
   b. Slide0
   c. Undefined
   d. Undefined

101. The _____ (symbol _____) and the millibar (symbol mbar, also mb) are units of pressure.
   a. Bar0
   b. Thing
   c. Undefined
   d. Undefined

102. A _____ is a method of using property as security for the payment of a debt.
   a. Mortgage0
   b. Thing
   c. Undefined
   d. Undefined

103. In mathematics, the conjugate _____ or adjoint matrix of an m-by-n matrix A with complex entries is the n-by-m matrix A* obtained from A by taking the transpose and then taking the complex conjugate of each entry.
   a. Pairs0
   b. Thing
   c. Undefined
   d. Undefined

104. A pair of angles are _____ if the sum of their angles is 90°.
   a. Complementary0
   b. Concept
   c. Undefined
   d. Undefined

105. A pair of angles is _____ if their respective measures sum to 180 degrees.
   a. Supplementary0
   b. Concept
   c. Undefined
   d. Undefined

106. In mathematics, an inequality is a statement about the relative size or order of two objects. For example 14 > 10, or 14 is _____ 10.
   a. Greater than0
   b. Thing
   c. Undefined
   d. Undefined

107. A _____ is one of the basic shapes of geometry: a polygon with three vertices and three sides which are straight line segments.
   a. Thing
   b. Triangle0
   c. Undefined
   d. Undefined

108. In finance and economics, _____ is the process of finding the present value of an amount of cash at some future date, and along with compounding cash forms the basis of time value of money calculations.

a. Thing
b. Discount0
c. Undefined
d. Undefined

109. In mathematics, a _____ function in the sense of algebraic geometry is an everywhere-defined, polynomial function on an algebraic variety V with values in the field K over which V is defined.
a. Thing
b. Regular0
c. Undefined
d. Undefined

110. _____ is the transport of people on a trip/journey or the process or time involved in a person or object moving from one location to another.
a. Thing
b. Travel0
c. Undefined
d. Undefined

111. _____ usually refers to money in the form of liquid currency, such as banknotes or coins.
a. Cash0
b. Thing
c. Undefined
d. Undefined

112. _____ are economic entities that give rise to future economic benefit and is controlled by the entity as a result of past transaction or other events
a. Asset0
b. Thing
c. Undefined
d. Undefined

113. U.S. liquid _____ is legally defined as 231 cubic inches, and is equal to 3.785411784 litres or abotu 0.13368 cubic feet. This is the most common definition of a _____. The U.S. fluid ounce is defined as 1/128 of a U.S. _____.
a. Gallon0
b. Thing
c. Undefined
d. Undefined

114. A _____ is a compensation which workers receive in exchange for their labor.
a. Wage0
b. Thing
c. Undefined
d. Undefined

115. _____, from Latin meaning "to make progress", is defined in two different ways. Pure economic _____ is the increase in wealth that an investor has from making an investment, taking into consideration all costs associated with that investment including the opportunity cost of capital.
a. Thing
b. Profit0
c. Undefined
d. Undefined

116. _____ is the distance around a given two-dimensional object. As a general rule, the _____ of a polygon can always be calculated by adding all the length of the sides together. So, the formula for triangles is P = a + b + c, where a, b and c stand for each side of it. For quadrilaterals the equation is P = a + b + c + d. For equilateral polygons, P = na, where n is the number of sides and a is the side length.
a. Thing
b. Perimeter0
c. Undefined
d. Undefined

Chapter 2. Equations and Inequalities

117. In mathematics, the additive inverse, or _____ of a number n is the number that, when added to n, yields zero. The additive inverse of n is denoted −n. For example, 7 is −7, because 7 + (−7) = 0, and the additive inverse of −0.3 is 0.3, because −0.3 + 0.3 = 0.
   a. Thing
   b. Opposite0
   c. Undefined
   d. Undefined

118. In mathematics, the _____ of a number n is the number that, when added to n, yields zero. The _____ of n is denoted −n. For example, 7 is −7, because 7 + (−7) = 0, and the _____ of −0.3 is 0.3, because −0.3 + 0.3 = 0.
   a. Thing
   b. Additive inverse0
   c. Undefined
   d. Undefined

119. An _____ is an angle formed by two sides of a simple polygon that share an endpoint, namely, the angle on the inner side of the polygon.
   a. Interior angle0
   b. Thing
   c. Undefined
   d. Undefined

120. Compass and straightedge or ruler-and-compass _____ is the _____ of lengths or angles using only an idealized ruler and compass.
   a. Construction0
   b. Thing
   c. Undefined
   d. Undefined

121. Sir Isaac _____, was an English physicist, mathematician, astronomer, natural philosopher, and alchemist, regarded by many as the greatest figure in the history of science
   a. Person
   b. Newton0
   c. Undefined
   d. Undefined

122. In mathematics, an _____, mean, or central tendency of a data set refers to a measure of the "middle" or "expected" value of the data set.
   a. Concept
   b. Average0
   c. Undefined
   d. Undefined

123. Acid _____ ratio measures the ability of a company to use its near cash or quick assets to immediately extinguish its current liabilities.
   a. Thing
   b. Test0
   c. Undefined
   d. Undefined

124. _____ are procedures that allow people to exchange information by one of several methods.
   a. Communications0
   b. Thing
   c. Undefined
   d. Undefined

125. In chemistry, a _____ is substance made by combining two or more different materials in such a way that no chemical reaction occurs.
   a. Thing
   b. Mixture0
   c. Undefined
   d. Undefined

Chapter 2. Equations and Inequalities

126. In banking and accountancy, the outstanding _____ is the amount of money owned, or due, that remains in a deposit account or a loan account at a given date, after all past remittances, payments and withdrawal have been accounted for.
 a. Balance0
 b. Thing
 c. Undefined
 d. Undefined

127. In geometry, an _____ of a triangle is a straight line through a vertex and perpendicular to (i.e. forming a right angle with) the opposite side or an extension of the opposite side.
 a. Altitude0
 b. Concept
 c. Undefined
 d. Undefined

128. In botany, _____ are above-ground plant organs specialized for photosynthesis. Their characteristics are typically analyzed by using Fiobonacci's sequences.
 a. Thing
 b. Leaves0
 c. Undefined
 d. Undefined

129. _____ is a state located in the southern and southwestern regions of the United States of America.
 a. Thing
 b. Texas0
 c. Undefined
 d. Undefined

130. _____, in economics and political economy, are the distributions or payments awarded to the various suppliers of the factors of production.
 a. Thing
 b. Returns0
 c. Undefined
 d. Undefined

131. In mathematics, the _____ of a function is the set of all "output" values produced by that function. Given a function $f : A \to B$, the _____ of f, is defined to be the set $\{x \in B : x = f(a) \text{ for some } a \in A\}$.
 a. Thing
 b. Range0
 c. Undefined
 d. Undefined

132. _____ is the portion of income that is the subject of taxation according to the laws that determine what is income and the taxation rate for that income.
 a. Taxable income0
 b. Thing
 c. Undefined
 d. Undefined

133. In physics, _____ is an influence that may cause an object to accelerate. It may be experienced as a lift, a push, or a pull. The actual acceleration of the body is determined by the vector sum of all forces acting on it, known as net _____ or resultant _____.
 a. Thing
 b. Force0
 c. Undefined
 d. Undefined

134. In mathematics, a _____ is a two-dimensional manifold or surface that is perfectly flat.
 a. Plane0
 b. Thing
 c. Undefined
 d. Undefined

135. Transport or _____ is the movement of people and goods from one place to another.

Chapter 2. Equations and Inequalities

  a. Thing
  b. Transportation0
  c. Undefined
  d. Undefined

136. A _____ is a vehicle, missile or aircraft which obtains thrust by the reaction to the ejection of fast moving fluid from within a _____ engine.
  a. Thing
  b. Rocket0
  c. Undefined
  d. Undefined

137. Mathematical _____ is used to represent ideas.
  a. Notation0
  b. Thing
  c. Undefined
  d. Undefined

138. In mathematics, a _____ is the end result of a division problem. It can also be expressed as the number of times the divisor divides into the dividend.
  a. Thing
  b. Quotient0
  c. Undefined
  d. Undefined

139. _____ is a notation for writing numbers that is often used by scientists and mathematicians to make it easier to write large and small numbers.
  a. Scientific notation0
  b. Thing
  c. Undefined
  d. Undefined

140. A _____ is a one-dimensional picture in which the integers are shown as specially-marked points evenly spaced on a line.
  a. Number line0
  b. Thing
  c. Undefined
  d. Undefined

141. In elementary algebra, an _____ is a set that contains every real number between two indicated numbers and may contain the two numbers themselves.
  a. Thing
  b. Interval0
  c. Undefined
  d. Undefined

142. _____ is the notation in which permitted values for a variable are expressed as ranging over a certain interval; "5 < x < 9" is an example of the application of _____.
  a. Thing
  b. Interval notation0
  c. Undefined
  d. Undefined

143. A _____ is a number that is less than zero.
  a. Thing
  b. Negative number0
  c. Undefined
  d. Undefined

144. In geometry, an _____ is a point at which a line segment or ray terminates.
  a. Thing
  b. Endpoint0
  c. Undefined
  d. Undefined

Chapter 2. Equations and Inequalities

145. In mathematics, _____ geometry was the traditional name for the geometry of three-dimensional Euclidean space — for practical purposes the kind of space we live in.
 a. Thing
 b. Solid0
 c. Undefined
 d. Undefined

146. _____ is the state of being greater than any finite number, however large.
 a. Infinity0
 b. Thing
 c. Undefined
 d. Undefined

147. _____ is a business term for the amount of money that a company receives from its activities in a given period, mostly from sales of products and/or services to customers
 a. Thing
 b. Revenue0
 c. Undefined
 d. Undefined

148. _____ is the starting form for personal individual Federal income tax returns filed with the Internal Revenue Service IRS in the United States.
 a. Thing
 b. Form 10400
 c. Undefined
 d. Undefined

149. In financial mathematics, the _____ volatility of an option contract is the volatility _____ by the market price of the option based on an option pricing model.
 a. Implied0
 b. Thing
 c. Undefined
 d. Undefined

150. An _____ or member of a set is an object that when collected together make up the set.
 a. Thing
 b. Element0
 c. Undefined
 d. Undefined

151. In mathematics, the _____ , or members of a set or more generally a class are all those objects which when collected together make up the set or class.
 a. Elements0
 b. Thing
 c. Undefined
 d. Undefined

152. In mathematics, the _____ of two sets A and B is the set that contains all elements of A that also belong to B (or equivalently, all elements of B that also belong to A), but no other elements.
 a. Intersection0
 b. Thing
 c. Undefined
 d. Undefined

153. _____ is a form of periodic payment from an employer to an employee, which is specified in an employment contract.
 a. Thing
 b. Gross pay0
 c. Undefined
 d. Undefined

154. A _____ is a form of periodic payment from an employer to an employee, which is specified in an employment contract.

a. Salary0
b. Thing
c. Undefined
d. Undefined

155. A _____ given two distinct points A and B on the _____, is the set of points C on the line containing points A and B such that A is not strictly between C and B.
   a. Thing
   b. Ray0
   c. Undefined
   d. Undefined

156. A _____ is an individual or household that purchases and uses goods and services generated within the economy.
   a. Thing
   b. Consumer0
   c. Undefined
   d. Undefined

157. _____ has many meanings, most of which simply .
   a. Thing
   b. Power0
   c. Undefined
   d. Undefined

158. In an insurance policy, the _____ or excess is the portion of any claim that is not covered by the insurance provider.
   a. Deductible0
   b. Thing
   c. Undefined
   d. Undefined

159. A _____ is a plan of action to guide decisions and actions.
   a. Policy0
   b. Thing
   c. Undefined
   d. Undefined

160. _____ is the mathematical action of repeatedly adding or subtracting one, usually to find out how many objects there are or to set aside a desired number of objects.
   a. Counting0
   b. Thing
   c. Undefined
   d. Undefined

161. _____ the expected value of a random variable displays the average or central value of the variable.It is a summary value of the distribution of the variable.
   a. Determining0
   b. Thing
   c. Undefined
   d. Undefined

162. In mathematics, a class _____ is a structure used to organize the various Galois groups and modules that appear in class field theory. They were invented by Emil Artin and John Tate.
   a. Formation0
   b. Thing
   c. Undefined
   d. Undefined

163. _____ is a Fortune 200 company, and the third largest consumer electronics retailer in the United States with over $11 billion USD in sales, behind Best Buy and Wal-Mart.
   a. Thing
   b. Circuit City0
   c. Undefined
   d. Undefined

Chapter 2. Equations and Inequalities

164. In geometry, a _____ (Greek words diairo = divide and metro = measure) of a circle is any straight line segment that passes through the centre and whose endpoints are on the circular boundary, or, in more modern usage, the length of such a line segment. When using the word in the more modern sense, one speaks of the _____ rather than a _____, because all diameters of a circle have the same length. This length is twice the radius. The _____ of a circle is also the longest chord that the circle has.
   a. Thing
   b. Diameter0
   c. Undefined
   d. Undefined

165. The _____ is a property of multiplication or addition where the product or sum remains the same, regardless of whether or not the order of the addends or factors are changed.
   a. Commutative property0
   b. Thing
   c. Undefined
   d. Undefined

166. _____ is the state of being greater than any finite real or natural number, however large.
   a. Infinite0
   b. Thing
   c. Undefined
   d. Undefined

167. In mathematics, _____ is a property that a binary operation can have. Within an expression containing two or more of the same associative operators in a row, the order of operations does not matter as long as the sequence of the operands is not changed.
   a. Associativity0
   b. Thing
   c. Undefined
   d. Undefined

Chapter 3. Graphs and Functions

1. An _____ or member of a set is an object that when collected together make up the set.
   a. Thing
   b. Element0
   c. Undefined
   d. Undefined

2. The mathematical concept of a _____ expresses the intuitive idea of deterministic dependence between two quantities, one of which is viewed as primary and the other as secondary. A _____ then is a way to associate a unique output for each input of a specified type, for example, a real number or an element of a given set.
   a. Thing
   b. Function0
   c. Undefined
   d. Undefined

3. A _____ is a set of numbers that designate location in a given reference system, such as x,y in a planar _____ system or an x,y,z in a three-dimensional _____ system.
   a. Coordinate0
   b. Thing
   c. Undefined
   d. Undefined

4. In mathematics and its applications, a _____ is a system for assigning an n-tuple of numbers or scalars to each point in an n-dimensional space.
   a. Coordinate system0
   b. Concept
   c. Undefined
   d. Undefined

5. _____ means of or relating to the French philosopher and mathematician René Descartes.
   a. Cartesian0
   b. Thing
   c. Undefined
   d. Undefined

6. In mathematics, the _____ is used to determine each point uniquely in a plane through two numbers, usually called the x-coordinate and the y-coordinate of the point.
   a. Cartesian coordinate system0
   b. Thing
   c. Undefined
   d. Undefined

7. A _____ is a symbolic representation denoting a quantity or expression. It often represents an "unknown" quantity that has the potential to change.
   a. Variable0
   b. Thing
   c. Undefined
   d. Undefined

8. A _____ is a one-dimensional picture in which the integers are shown as specially-marked points evenly spaced on a line.
   a. Number line0
   b. Thing
   c. Undefined
   d. Undefined

9. An _____ is when two lines intersect somewhere on a plane creating a right angle at intersection
   a. Thing
   b. Axes0
   c. Undefined
   d. Undefined

10. In geometry, two lines or planes if one falls on the other in such a way as to create congruent adjacent angles. The term may be used as a noun or adjective. Thus, referring to Figure 1, the line AB is the _____ to CD through the point B.

Chapter 3. Graphs and Functions

a. Perpendicular0
b. Thing
c. Undefined
d. Undefined

11. In mathematics, a _____ is a two-dimensional manifold or surface that is perfectly flat.
a. Thing
b. Plane0
c. Undefined
d. Undefined

12. _____ was a highly influential French philosopher, mathematician, scientist, and writer. Dubbed the "Founder of Modern Philosophy", and the "Father of Modern Mathematics". His theories provided the basis for the calculus of Newton and Leibniz, by applying infinitesimal calculus to the tangent line problem, thus permitting the evolution of that branch of modern mathematics
a. Person
b. Descartes0
c. Undefined
d. Undefined

13. A _____ consists of one quarter of the coordinate plane.
a. Quadrant0
b. Thing
c. Undefined
d. Undefined

14. A _____ is a symbol or group of symbols, or a word in a natural language that represents a number.
a. Thing
b. Numeral0
c. Undefined
d. Undefined

15. An _____ is a straight line around which a geometric figure can be rotated.
a. Axis0
b. Thing
c. Undefined
d. Undefined

16. In astronomy, geography, geometry and related sciences and contexts, a plane is said to be _____ at a given point if it is locally perpendicular to the gradient of the gravity field, i.e., with the direction of the gravitational force at that point.
a. Horizontal0
b. Thing
c. Undefined
d. Undefined

17. _____ numerals are a numeral system originating in ancient Rome, adapted from Etruscan numerals.
a. Thing
b. Roman0
c. Undefined
d. Undefined

18. In mathematics, the _____ of a coordinate system is the point where the axes of the system intersect.
a. Origin0
b. Thing
c. Undefined
d. Undefined

19. In mathematics, the _____ of two sets A and B is the set that contains all elements of A that also belong to B (or equivalently, all elements of B that also belong to A), but no other elements.
a. Intersection0
b. Thing
c. Undefined
d. Undefined

20. _____ are the basic objects of study in graph theory. Informally speaking, a graph is a set of objects called points, nodes, or vertices connected by links called lines or edges.

Chapter 3. Graphs and Functions

   a. Thing
   b. Graphs0
   c. Undefined
   d. Undefined

21. An _____ is a collection of two not necessarily distinct objects, one of which is distinguished as the first coordinate and the other as the second coordinate.
   a. Thing
   b. Ordered pair0
   c. Undefined
   d. Undefined

22. In mathematics, an _____ number is a complex number whose square is a negative real number. They were defined in 1572 by Rafael Bombelli.
   a. Thing
   b. Imaginary0
   c. Undefined
   d. Undefined

23. In mathematics, the conjugate _____ or adjoint matrix of an m-by-n matrix A with complex entries is the n-by-m matrix A* obtained from A by taking the transpose and then taking the complex conjugate of each entry.
   a. Thing
   b. Pairs0
   c. Undefined
   d. Undefined

24. In common philosophical language, a proposition or _____, is the content of an assertion, that is, it is true-or-false and defined by the meaning of a particular piece of language.
   a. Statement0
   b. Concept
   c. Undefined
   d. Undefined

25. _____ is the state of being greater than any finite real or natural number, however large.
   a. Infinite0
   b. Thing
   c. Undefined
   d. Undefined

26. Three or more points that lie on the same line are called _____.
   a. Collinear0
   b. Thing
   c. Undefined
   d. Undefined

27. The word _____ comes from the Latin word linearis, which means created by lines.
   a. Linear0
   b. Thing
   c. Undefined
   d. Undefined

28. A _____ is an equation in which each term is either a constant or the product of a constant times the first power of a variable.
   a. Thing
   b. Linear equation0
   c. Undefined
   d. Undefined

29. The _____ of a ring R is defined to be the smallest positive integer n such that n a = 0, for all a in R.
   a. Thing
   b. Characteristic0
   c. Undefined
   d. Undefined

30. _____ is the study of terms and their use — of words and compound words that are used in specific contexts.

Chapter 3. Graphs and Functions 37

a. Terminology0
b. Thing
c. Undefined
d. Undefined

31. Acid _____ ratio measures the ability of a company to use its near cash or quick assets to immediately extinguish its current liabilities.
   a. Test0
   b. Thing
   c. Undefined
   d. Undefined

32. A _____ is a tool similar to a ruler, but without markings.
   a. Thing
   b. Straightedge0
   c. Undefined
   d. Undefined

33. A _____ is an instrument used in geometry technical drawing and engineering/building to measure distances and/or to rule straight lines.
   a. Thing
   b. Ruler0
   c. Undefined
   d. Undefined

34. In Euclidean geometry, a uniform _____ is a linear transformation that enlargers or diminishes objects, and whose _____ factor is the same in all directions. This is also called homothethy.
   a. Scale0
   b. Thing
   c. Undefined
   d. Undefined

35. A _____ is a negotiable instrument instructing a financial institution to pay a specific amount of a specific currency from a specific demand account held in the maker/depositor's name with that institution. Both the maker and payee may be natural persons or legal entities.
   a. Thing
   b. Check0
   c. Undefined
   d. Undefined

36. A _____ of a number is the product of that number with any integer.
   a. Multiple0
   b. Thing
   c. Undefined
   d. Undefined

37. _____ systems represent systems whose behavior is not expressible as a sum of the behaviors of its descriptors.
   a. Nonlinear0
   b. Thing
   c. Undefined
   d. Undefined

38. In mathematics, defined and _____ are used to explain whether or not expressions have meaningful, sensible, and unambiguous values.
   a. Thing
   b. Undefined0
   c. Undefined
   d. Undefined

39. In mathematics, the _____ (or modulus) of a real number is its numerical value without regard to its sign.
   a. Thing
   b. Absolute value0
   c. Undefined
   d. Undefined

Chapter 3. Graphs and Functions

40. A _____ is the part of a fraction that tells how many equal parts make up a whole, and which is used in the name of the fraction: "halves", "thirds", "fourths" or "quarters", "fifths" and so on.
    a. Concept
    b. Denominator0
    c. Undefined
    d. Undefined

41. In geographic information systems, a _____ comprises an entity with a geographic location, typically determined by points, arcs, or polygons. Carriageways and cadastres exemplify _____ data.
    a. Feature0
    b. Thing
    c. Undefined
    d. Undefined

42. _____ are objects, characters, or other concrete representations of ideas, concepts, or other abstractions.
    a. Symbols0
    b. Thing
    c. Undefined
    d. Undefined

43. In linear algebra, the _____ of an n-by-n square matrix A is defined to be the sum of the elements on the main diagonal of A,
    a. Trace0
    b. Thing
    c. Undefined
    d. Undefined

44. _____ are a measure of time.
    a. Thing
    b. Minutes0
    c. Undefined
    d. Undefined

45. A _____ is a unit of length, usually used to measure distance, in a number of different systems, including Imperial units, United States customary units and Norwegian/Swedish mil. Its size can vary from system to system, but in each is between 1 and 10 kilometers. In contemporary English contexts _____ refers to either:
    a. Thing
    b. Mile0
    c. Undefined
    d. Undefined

46. _____ is a unit of speed, expressing the number of international miles covered per hour.
    a. Thing
    b. Miles per hour0
    c. Undefined
    d. Undefined

47. In geometry, a line _____ is a part of a line that is bounded by two end points, and contains every point on the line between its end points.
    a. Segment0
    b. Concept
    c. Undefined
    d. Undefined

48. A _____ is a part of a line that is bounded by two end points, and contains every point on the line between its end points.
    a. Line segment0
    b. Thing
    c. Undefined
    d. Undefined

49. A _____ is a special kind of ratio, indicating a relationship between two measurements with different units, such as miles to gallons or cents to pounds.

Chapter 3. Graphs and Functions

  a. Rate0
  b. Thing
  c. Undefined
  d. Undefined

50. In mathematics, a matrix can be thought of as each row or _____ being a vector. Hence, a space formed by row vectors or _____ vectors are said to be a row space or a _____ space.
  a. Column0
  b. Concept
  c. Undefined
  d. Undefined

51. A _____ (symbol ha) is a unit of area, equal to 10,000 square metres, commonly used for measuring land area. Its base unit, the are, was defined by older forms of the metric system, but neither it nor the _____ are part of the modern metric system.
  a. Hectare0
  b. Concept
  c. Undefined
  d. Undefined

52. In mathematics a _____ is a function which defines a distance between elements of a set.
  a. Metric0
  b. Thing
  c. Undefined
  d. Undefined

53. The _____ is a decimalized system of measurement based on the metre and the gram.
  a. Metric system0
  b. Concept
  c. Undefined
  d. Undefined

54. The _____ of measurement are a globally standardized and modernized form of the metric system.
  a. Thing
  b. Units0
  c. Undefined
  d. Undefined

55. The _____ of a geographic location is its height above a fixed reference point, often the mean sea level.
  a. Thing
  b. Elevation0
  c. Undefined
  d. Undefined

56. In mathematics, _____ refers to a number of loosely related concepts in different areas of geometry. Intuitively, _____ is the amount by which a geometric object deviates from being flat, but this is defined in different ways depending on the context
  a. Thing
  b. Curvature0
  c. Undefined
  d. Undefined

57. _____ is the middle point of a line segment.
  a. Midpoint0
  b. Thing
  c. Undefined
  d. Undefined

58. A _____ is a four-sided plane figure that has two sets of opposite parallel sides.
  a. Concept
  b. Parallelogram0
  c. Undefined
  d. Undefined

59. Mathematical _____ is used to represent ideas.

a. Thing
b. Notation0
c. Undefined
d. Undefined

60. In mathematics, an _____ is a statement about the relative size or order of two objects.
    a. Inequality0
    b. Thing
    c. Undefined
    d. Undefined

61. In geometry, the _____ of an object is a point in some sense in the middle of the object.
    a. Thing
    b. Center0
    c. Undefined
    d. Undefined

62. In mathematics, an _____ is any of the arguments, i.e. "inputs", to a function. Thus if we have a function f(x), then x is a _____.
    a. Independent variable0
    b. Thing
    c. Undefined
    d. Undefined

63. In a function the _____, is the variable which is the value, i.e. the "output", of the function.
    a. Thing
    b. Dependent variable0
    c. Undefined
    d. Undefined

64. In mathematics, a _____ of a k-place relation $L \subseteq X_1 \times ... \times X_k$ is one of the sets X_j, $1 \leq j \leq k$. In the special case where k = 2 and $L \subseteq X_1 \times X_2$ is a function $L : X_1 \to X_2$, it is conventional to refer to X_1 as the _____ of the function and to refer to X_2 as the codomain of the function.
    a. Domain0
    b. Thing
    c. Undefined
    d. Undefined

65. In mathematics, the _____ of a function is the set of all "output" values produced by that function. Given a function $f : A \to B$, the _____ of f, is defined to be the set $\{x \in B : x = f(a) \text{ for some } a \in A\}$.
    a. Range0
    b. Thing
    c. Undefined
    d. Undefined

66. In mathematics, the _____ , or members of a set or more generally a class are all those objects which when collected together make up the set or class.
    a. Thing
    b. Elements0
    c. Undefined
    d. Undefined

67. _____ is a test to determine if a relation or its graph is a function or not
    a. Vertical line test0
    b. Thing
    c. Undefined
    d. Undefined

68. In mathematics, the _____ f is the collection of all ordered pairs . In particular, graph means the graphical representation of this collection, in the form of a curve or surface, together with axes, etc. Graphing on a Cartesian plane is sometimes referred to as curve sketching.
    a. Thing
    b. Graph of a function0
    c. Undefined
    d. Undefined

Chapter 3. Graphs and Functions

69. In mathematics, a _____ may be described informally as a number that can be given by an infinite decimal representation.
    a. Thing
    b. Real number0
    c. Undefined
    d. Undefined

70. In mathematics, an inequality is a statement about the relative size or order of two objects. For example 14 > 10, or 14 is _____ 10.
    a. Greater than0
    b. Thing
    c. Undefined
    d. Undefined

71. The _____, the average in everyday English, which is also called the arithmetic _____ (and is distinguished from the geometric _____ or harmonic _____). The average is also called the sample _____. The expected value of a random variable, which is also called the population _____.
    a. Thing
    b. Mean0
    c. Undefined
    d. Undefined

72. In mathematics and the mathematical sciences, a _____ is a fixed, but possibly unspecified, value. This is in contrast to a variable, which is not fixed.
    a. Thing
    b. Constant0
    c. Undefined
    d. Undefined

73. In Euclidean geometry, a _____ is the set of all points in a plane at a fixed distance, called the radius, from a given point, the center.
    a. Circle0
    b. Thing
    c. Undefined
    d. Undefined

74. In mathematics, an _____ .
    a. Thing
    b. Ellipse0
    c. Undefined
    d. Undefined

75. _____ is a state in the southern region of the United States of America and was one of the original Thirteen Colonies that revolted against British rule in the American Revolution.
    a. Georgia0
    b. Thing
    c. Undefined
    d. Undefined

76. _____ is a way of expressing a number as a fraction of 100 per cent meaning "per hundred".
    a. Percent0
    b. Thing
    c. Undefined
    d. Undefined

77. In business, particularly accounting, a _____ is the time intervals that the accounts, statement, payments, or other calculations cover.
    a. Period0
    b. Thing
    c. Undefined
    d. Undefined

78. _____ is a kind of property which exists as magnitude or multitude. It is among the basic classes of things along with quality, substance, change, and relation.

a. Thing
c. Undefined
b. Amount0
d. Undefined

79. A _____ is a deliberate process for transforming one or more inputs into one or more results.
    a. Thing
    c. Undefined
    b. Calculation0
    d. Undefined

80. In sociology and biology a _____ is the collection of people or organisms of a particular species living in a given geographic area or space, usually measured by a census.
    a. Thing
    c. Undefined
    b. Population0
    d. Undefined

81. In geometry, a _____ is defined as a quadrilateral where all four of its angles are right angles.
    a. Thing
    c. Undefined
    b. Rectangle0
    d. Undefined

82. _____ is the fee paid on borrowed money.
    a. Thing
    c. Undefined
    b. Interest0
    d. Undefined

83. An _____ is the fee paid on borrow money.
    a. Interest rate0
    c. Undefined
    b. Concept
    d. Undefined

84. In plane geometry, a _____ is a polygon with four equal sides, four right angles, and parallel opposite sides. In algebra, the _____ of a number is that number multiplied by itself.
    a. Thing
    c. Undefined
    b. Square0
    d. Undefined

85. _____ is the distance around a given two-dimensional object. As a general rule, the _____ of a polygon can always be calculated by adding all the length of the sides together. So, the formula for triangles is P = a + b + c, where a, b and c stand for each side of it. For quadrilaterals the equation is P = a + b + c + d. For equilateral polygons, P = na, where n is the number of sides and a is the side length.
    a. Perimeter0
    c. Undefined
    b. Thing
    d. Undefined

86. _____ is a temperature scale named after the German physicist Daniel Gabriel _____ , who proposed it in 1724.
    a. Thing
    c. Undefined
    b. Fahrenheit0
    d. Undefined

87. _____ is, or relates to, the _____ temperature scale .
    a. Celsius0
    c. Undefined
    b. Thing
    d. Undefined

Chapter 3. Graphs and Functions

88. _____ is a physical property of a system that underlies the common notions of hot and cold; something that is hotter has the greater _____.
   a. Thing
   b. Temperature0
   c. Undefined
   d. Undefined

89. An n-sided _____ is a polyhedron formed by connecting an n-sided polygonal base and a point, called the apex, by n triangular faces. In other words, it is a conic solid with polygonal base.
   a. Thing
   b. Pyramid0
   c. Undefined
   d. Undefined

90. _____ is a business term for the amount of money that a company receives from its activities in a given period, mostly from sales of products and/or services to customers
   a. Revenue0
   b. Thing
   c. Undefined
   d. Undefined

91. The _____ of a solid object is the three-dimensional concept of how much space it occupies, often quantified numerically.
   a. Thing
   b. Volume0
   c. Undefined
   d. Undefined

92. In classical geometry, a _____ of a circle or sphere is any line segment from its center to its boundary. By extension, the _____ of a circle or sphere is the length of any such segment. The _____ is half the diameter. In science and engineering the term _____ of curvature is commonly used as a synonym for _____.
   a. Radius0
   b. Thing
   c. Undefined
   d. Undefined

93. In mathematics, there are several meanings of _____ depending on the subject.
   a. Degree0
   b. Thing
   c. Undefined
   d. Undefined

94. A _____ is 360° or 2∂ radians.
   a. Turn0
   b. Thing
   c. Undefined
   d. Undefined

95. _____ is the transport of people on a trip/journey or the process or time involved in a person or object moving from one location to another.
   a. Travel0
   b. Thing
   c. Undefined
   d. Undefined

96. In mathematics, an _____, mean, or central tendency of a data set refers to a measure of the "middle" or "expected" value of the data set.
   a. Concept
   b. Average0
   c. Undefined
   d. Undefined

97. In economics, supply and _____ describe market relations between prospective sellers and buyers of a good.

Chapter 3. Graphs and Functions

a. Demand0
b. Thing
c. Undefined
d. Undefined

98. A _____ defined function f(x) of a real variable x is a function whose definition is given differently on disjoint subsets of its domain.
    a. Thing
    b. Piecewise0
    c. Undefined
    d. Undefined

99. A _____ is a first degree polynomial mathematical function of the form: f(x) = mx + b where m and b are real constants and x is a real variable.
    a. Thing
    b. Linear function0
    c. Undefined
    d. Undefined

100. Any point where a graph makes contact with an coordinate axis is called an _____ of the graph
    a. Intercept0
    b. Thing
    c. Undefined
    d. Undefined

101. _____ is a notation for writing numbers that is often used by scientists and mathematicians to make it easier to write large and small numbers.
    a. Scientific notation0
    b. Thing
    c. Undefined
    d. Undefined

102. In mathematics, and in particular in abstract algebra, the _____ is a property of binary operations that generalises the distributive law from elementary algebra.
    a. Distributive property0
    b. Thing
    c. Undefined
    d. Undefined

103. In mathematics, a _____ of a complex-valued function f is a member x of the domain of f such that f(x) vanishes at x, that is, x : f (x) = 0.
    a. Root0
    b. Thing
    c. Undefined
    d. Undefined

104. In mathematics, the concept of a _____ tries to capture the intuitive idea of a geometrical one-dimensional and continuous object. A simple example is the circle.
    a. Thing
    b. Curve0
    c. Undefined
    d. Undefined

105. _____, from Latin meaning "to make progress", is defined in two different ways. Pure economic _____ is the increase in wealth that an investor has from making an investment, taking into consideration all costs associated with that investment including the opportunity cost of capital.
    a. Thing
    b. Profit0
    c. Undefined
    d. Undefined

106. _____ the expected value of a random variable displays the average or central value of the variable. It is a summary value of the distribution of the variable.

Chapter 3. Graphs and Functions

a. Determining0
c. Undefined
b. Thing
d. Undefined

107. _____ is a form of periodic payment from an employer to an employee, which is specified in an employment contract.
   a. Thing
   b. Gross pay0
   c. Undefined
   d. Undefined

108. A _____ is a form of periodic payment from an employer to an employee, which is specified in an employment contract.
   a. Thing
   b. Salary0
   c. Undefined
   d. Undefined

109. In geometry, the relations of _____ are those such as 'lies on' between points and lines (as in 'point P lies on line L'), and 'intersects' (as in 'line L_1 intersects line L_2', in three-dimensional space). That is, they are the binary relations describing how subsets meet.
   a. Thing
   b. Incidence0
   c. Undefined
   d. Undefined

110. _____ interest refers to the fact that whenever interest is calculated, it is based not only on the original principal, but also on any unpaid interest that has been added to the principal.
   a. Thing
   b. Compound0
   c. Undefined
   d. Undefined

111. In geometry, a _____ (Greek words diairo = divide and metro = measure) of a circle is any straight line segment that passes through the centre and whose endpoints are on the circular boundary, or, in more modern usage, the length of such a line segment. When using the word in the more modern sense, one speaks of the _____ rather than a _____, because all diameters of a circle have the same length. This length is twice the radius. The _____ of a circle is also the longest chord that the circle has.
   a. Thing
   b. Diameter0
   c. Undefined
   d. Undefined

112. _____ is the level of functional and/or metabolic efficiency of an organism at both the micro level.
   a. Health0
   b. Thing
   c. Undefined
   d. Undefined

113. In mathematics, factorization (British English: factorisation) or factoring is the decomposition of an object (for example, a number, a polynomial, or a matrix) into a product of other objects, or _____, which when multiplied together give the original.
   a. Thing
   b. Factors0
   c. Undefined
   d. Undefined

114. _____ Any process by which a specified characteristic usually amplitude of the output of a device is prevented from exceeding a predetermined value.

a. Limiting0
b. Thing
c. Undefined
d. Undefined

115. A _____ is a plan of action to guide decisions and actions.
   a. Thing
   b. Policy0
   c. Undefined
   d. Undefined

116. _____ are the recurring expenses which are related to the operation of a business, or to the operation of a device, component, piece of equipment or facility.
   a. Operating cost0
   b. Thing
   c. Undefined
   d. Undefined

117. In Graph theory, a _____ is a digraph with weighted edges.
   a. Concept
   b. Network0
   c. Undefined
   d. Undefined

118. The payment of _____ as remuneration for services rendered or products sold is a common way to reward sales people.
   a. Thing
   b. Commission0
   c. Undefined
   d. Undefined

119. _____ is a mathematical science pertaining to the collection, analysis, interpretation or explanation, and presentation of data. It is applicable to a wide variety of academic disciplines, from the physical and social sciences to the humanities.
   a. Statistics0
   b. Thing
   c. Undefined
   d. Undefined

120. _____ is often used to describe the measurement of the steepness, incline, gradient, or grade of a straight line. The _____ is defined as the ratio of the "rise" divided by the "run" between two points on a line, or in other words, the ratio of the altitude change to the horizontal distance between any two points on the line.
   a. Slope0
   b. Thing
   c. Undefined
   d. Undefined

121. In Euclidean geometry, a _____ is moving every point a constant distance in a specified direction.
   a. Translation0
   b. Concept
   c. Undefined
   d. Undefined

122. A _____ is a quantity that denotes the proportional amount or magnitude of one quantity relative to another.
   a. Ratio0
   b. Thing
   c. Undefined
   d. Undefined

123. A _____ is an abstract model that uses mathematical language to describe the behavior of a system. Eykhoff defined a _____ as 'a representation of the essential aspects of an existing system which presents knowledge of that system in usable form'.

a. Mathematical model0
b. Thing
c. Undefined
d. Undefined

124. _____ forms part of thinking. Considered the most complex of all intellectual functions, _____ has been defined as higher-order cognitive process that requires the modulation and control of more routine or fundamental skills.
   a. Problem solving0
   b. Thing
   c. Undefined
   d. Undefined

125. _____ has many meanings, most of which simply .
   a. Power0
   b. Thing
   c. Undefined
   d. Undefined

126. A frame of _____ is a particular perspective from which the universe is observed.
   a. Reference0
   b. Thing
   c. Undefined
   d. Undefined

127. _____ is a synonym for information.
   a. Thing
   b. Data0
   c. Undefined
   d. Undefined

128. In probability theory and statistics, a _____ is a number dividing the higher half of a sample, a population, or a probability distribution from the lower half.
   a. Median0
   b. Concept
   c. Undefined
   d. Undefined

129. _____ primarily refers to social welfare service concerned with social protection, or protection against socially recognized conditions, including poverty, old age, disability, unemployment, families with children and others.
   a. Social security0
   b. Thing
   c. Undefined
   d. Undefined

130. Initial objects are also called _____, and terminal objects are also called final.
   a. Thing
   b. Coterminal0
   c. Undefined
   d. Undefined

131. In trigonometry, the _____ is a function defined as tan x = $^{\sin x}/_{\cos x}$. The function is so-named because it can be defined as the length of a certain segment of a _____ (in the geometric sense) to the unit circle. In plane geometry, a line is _____ to a curve, at some point, if both line and curve pass through the point with the same direction.
   a. Thing
   b. Tangent0
   c. Undefined
   d. Undefined

132. _____ has two distinct but etymologically-related meanings: one in geometry and one in trigonometry.
   a. Thing
   b. Tangent line0
   c. Undefined
   d. Undefined

133. _____ is a term used in accounting, economics and finance with reference to the fact that assets with finite lives lose value over time.

a. Thing
b. Depreciation0
c. Undefined
d. Undefined

134. The existence and properties of _____ are the basis of Euclid's parallel postulate. _____ are two lines on the same plane that do not intersect even assuming that lines extend to infinity in either direction.
   a. Parallel lines0
   b. Thing
   c. Undefined
   d. Undefined

135. In mathematics, the multiplicative inverse of a number x, denoted 1/x or x^{-1}, is the number which, when multiplied by x, yields 1. The multiplicative inverse of x is also called the _____ of x.
   a. Thing
   b. Reciprocal0
   c. Undefined
   d. Undefined

136. In mathematics, a _____ is the result of multiplying, or an expression that identifies factors to be multiplied.
   a. Thing
   b. Product0
   c. Undefined
   d. Undefined

137. _____ are a set of equations containing multiple variables.
   a. Thing
   b. Systems of equations0
   c. Undefined
   d. Undefined

138. In geometry a _____, or deltoid, is a quadrilateral with two pairs of congruent adjacent sides.
   a. Kite0
   b. Thing
   c. Undefined
   d. Undefined

139. U.S. liquid _____ is legally defined as 231 cubic inches, and is equal to 3.785411784 litres or abotu 0.13368 cubic feet. This is the most common definition of a _____. The U.S. fluid ounce is defined as 1/128 of a U.S. _____.
   a. Thing
   b. Gallon0
   c. Undefined
   d. Undefined

140. In descriptive statistics, using the _____ is a way of providing estimation of proportions of the data that should fall above and below a given value.
   a. Thing
   b. Percentile0
   c. Undefined
   d. Undefined

141. The _____ is the distance around a closed curve. _____ is a kind of perimeter.
   a. Thing
   b. Circumference0
   c. Undefined
   d. Undefined

142. _____ is a branch of mathematics concerning the study of structure, relation and quantity.
   a. Algebra0
   b. Concept
   c. Undefined
   d. Undefined

143. In mathematics, a _____ is the end result of a division problem. It can also be expressed as the number of times the divisor divides into the dividend.

Chapter 3. Graphs and Functions

a. Thing
b. Quotient0
c. Undefined
d. Undefined

144. A _____ is the result of the addition of a set of numbers. The numbers may be natural numbers, complex numbers, matrices, or still more complicated objects. An infinite _____ is a subtle procedure known as a series.
a. Thing
b. Sum0
c. Undefined
d. Undefined

145. In mathematics, _____ is an elementary arithmetic operation. When one of the numbers is a whole number, _____ is the repeated sum of the other number.
a. Multiplication0
b. Thing
c. Undefined
d. Undefined

146. In mathematics, _____ geometry was the traditional name for the geometry of three-dimensional Euclidean space — for practical purposes the kind of space we live in.
a. Solid0
b. Thing
c. Undefined
d. Undefined

147. _____ or life assurance is a contract between the policy owner and the insurer, where the insurer agrees to pay a sum of money upon the occurrence of the policy owner's death.
a. Life insurance0
b. Thing
c. Undefined
d. Undefined

148. _____, in law and economics, is a form of risk management primarily used to hedge against the risk of a contingent loss.
a. Insurance0
b. Thing
c. Undefined
d. Undefined

149. A _____ is an individual or household that purchases and uses goods and services generated within the economy.
a. Thing
b. Consumer0
c. Undefined
d. Undefined

150. _____ is a statistical time-series measure of a weighted average of prices of a specified set of goods and services purchased by consumers
a. Consumer price index0
b. Thing
c. Undefined
d. Undefined

151. The word _____ is used in a variety of ways in mathematics.
a. Index0
b. Thing
c. Undefined
d. Undefined

152. In mainstream economics, the word _____ refers to a general rise in prices measured against a standard level of purchasing power.

a. Thing
b. Inflation0
c. Undefined
d. Undefined

153. A _____ is a function that assigns a number to subsets of a given set.
a. Thing
b. Measure0
c. Undefined
d. Undefined

154. _____ is the production of food, feed, fiber, fuel and other goods by the systematic raizing of plants and animals.
a. Thing
b. Agriculture0
c. Undefined
d. Undefined

155. In mathematical analysis and related areas of mathematics, a set is called _____, if it is, in a certain sense, of finite size.
a. Thing
b. Bounded0
c. Undefined
d. Undefined

156. A _____ is a type of debt. All material things can be lent but this article focuses exclusively on monetary loans. Like all debt instruments, a _____ entails the redistribution of financial assets over time, between the lender and the borrower.
a. Loan0
b. Thing
c. Undefined
d. Undefined

157. In mathematics, a _____ is any one of several different types of functions, mappings, operations, or transformations.
a. Thing
b. Projection0
c. Undefined
d. Undefined

158. _____ studies and addresses the ways in which individuals, businesses, and organizations raise, allocate, and use monetary resources over time, taking into account the risks entailed in their projects
a. Finance0
b. Thing
c. Undefined
d. Undefined

159. A _____ is a set of possible values that a variable can take on in order to satisfy a given set of conditions, which may include equations and inequalities.
a. Thing
b. Solution set0
c. Undefined
d. Undefined

160. Compass and straightedge or ruler-and-compass _____ is the _____ of lengths or angles using only an idealized ruler and compass.
a. Construction0
b. Thing
c. Undefined
d. Undefined

Chapter 4. Systems of Equations and Inequalities

1. The word _____ comes from the Latin word linearis, which means created by lines.
   a. Thing
   b. Linear0
   c. Undefined
   d. Undefined

2. A _____ is an equation in which each term is either a constant or the product of a constant times the first power of a variable.
   a. Thing
   b. Linear equation0
   c. Undefined
   d. Undefined

3. A _____ is a negotiable instrument instructing a financial institution to pay a specific amount of a specific currency from a specific demand account held in the maker/depositor's name with that institution. Both the maker and payee may be natural persons or legal entities.
   a. Thing
   b. Check0
   c. Undefined
   d. Undefined

4. An _____ is a collection of two not necessarily distinct objects, one of which is distinguished as the first coordinate and the other as the second coordinate.
   a. Ordered pair0
   b. Thing
   c. Undefined
   d. Undefined

5. In mathematics, a _____ is an n-tuple with n being 3.
   a. Thing
   b. Triple0
   c. Undefined
   d. Undefined

6. A _____ is a symbolic representation denoting a quantity or expression. It often represents an "unknown" quantity that has the potential to change.
   a. Variable0
   b. Thing
   c. Undefined
   d. Undefined

7. An _____ is when two lines intersect somewhere on a plane creating a right angle at intersection
   a. Thing
   b. Axes0
   c. Undefined
   d. Undefined

8. In mathematics, the conjugate _____ or adjoint matrix of an m-by-n matrix A with complex entries is the n-by-m matrix A* obtained from A by taking the transpose and then taking the complex conjugate of each entry.
   a. Pairs0
   b. Thing
   c. Undefined
   d. Undefined

9. In mathematics, the _____ of two sets A and B is the set that contains all elements of A that also belong to B (or equivalently, all elements of B that also belong to A), but no other elements.
   a. Thing
   b. Intersection0
   c. Undefined
   d. Undefined

10. _____ is the state of being greater than any finite real or natural number, however large.
    a. Infinite0
    b. Thing
    c. Undefined
    d. Undefined

Chapter 4. Systems of Equations and Inequalities

11. _____ is often used to describe the measurement of the steepness, incline, gradient, or grade of a straight line. The _____ is defined as the ratio of the "rise" divided by the "run" between two points on a line, or in other words, the ratio of the altitude change to the horizontal distance between any two points on the line.
   a. Slope0
   b. Thing
   c. Undefined
   d. Undefined

12. _____ are the basic objects of study in graph theory. Informally speaking, a graph is a set of objects called points, nodes, or vertices connected by links called lines or edges.
   a. Graphs0
   b. Thing
   c. Undefined
   d. Undefined

13. The _____ is used to discard one of the variables in an equation, only to replace it with the actual value when solving multiple equations.
   a. Substitution method0
   b. Thing
   c. Undefined
   d. Undefined

14. An _____ is a combination of numbers, operators, grouping symbols and/or free variables and bound variables arranged in a meaningful way which can be evaluated..
   a. Thing
   b. Expression0
   c. Undefined
   d. Undefined

15. A _____ is the result of the addition of a set of numbers. The numbers may be natural numbers, complex numbers, matrices, or still more complicated objects. An infinite _____ is a subtle procedure known as a series.
   a. Thing
   b. Sum0
   c. Undefined
   d. Undefined

16. _____ is a notation for writing numbers that is often used by scientists and mathematicians to make it easier to write large and small numbers.
   a. Thing
   b. Scientific notation0
   c. Undefined
   d. Undefined

17. In mathematics and the mathematical sciences, a _____ is a fixed, but possibly unspecified, value. This is in contrast to a variable, which is not fixed.
   a. Constant0
   b. Thing
   c. Undefined
   d. Undefined

18. _____, either of the curved-bracket punctuation marks that together make a set of _____
   a. Parentheses0
   b. Thing
   c. Undefined
   d. Undefined

19. In mathematics, a _____ is an algebraic structure in which addition and multiplication are defined and have properties listed below.
   a. Ring0
   b. Thing
   c. Undefined
   d. Undefined

Chapter 4. Systems of Equations and Inequalities

20. Regrouping is the act of putting ones into groups of 10. For example, the 1 on the far right of 131 would be denoted _____ if the digit of the number being subtracted is larger than 1, such as 131-99.
    a. By 100
    b. Thing
    c. Undefined
    d. Undefined

21. A _____ is the part of a fraction that tells how many equal parts make up a whole, and which is used in the name of the fraction: "halves", "thirds", "fourths" or "quarters", "fifths" and so on.
    a. Denominator0
    b. Concept
    c. Undefined
    d. Undefined

22. In common philosophical language, a proposition or _____, is the content of an assertion, that is, it is true-or-false and defined by the meaning of a particular piece of language.
    a. Concept
    b. Statement0
    c. Undefined
    d. Undefined

23. The existence and properties of _____ are the basis of Euclid's parallel postulate. _____ are two lines on the same plane that do not intersect even assuming that lines extend to infinity in either direction.
    a. Parallel lines0
    b. Thing
    c. Undefined
    d. Undefined

24. In mathematics, a _____ is a constant multiplicative factor of a certain object. The object can be such things as a variable, a vector, a function, etc. For example, the _____ of $9x^2$ is 9.
    a. Thing
    b. Coefficient0
    c. Undefined
    d. Undefined

25. _____ forms part of thinking. Considered the most complex of all intellectual functions, _____ has been defined as higher-order cognitive process that requires the modulation and control of more routine or fundamental skills.
    a. Thing
    b. Problem solving0
    c. Undefined
    d. Undefined

26. In mathematics, an _____, mean, or central tendency of a data set refers to a measure of the "middle" or "expected" value of the data set.
    a. Average0
    b. Concept
    c. Undefined
    d. Undefined

27. The mathematical concept of a _____ expresses the intuitive idea of deterministic dependence between two quantities, one of which is viewed as primary and the other as secondary. A _____ then is a way to associate a unique output for each input of a specified type, for example, a real number or an element of a given set.
    a. Function0
    b. Thing
    c. Undefined
    d. Undefined

28. A _____ is a set of numbers that designate location in a given reference system, such as x,y in a planar _____ system or an x,y,z in a three-dimensional _____ system.
    a. Thing
    b. Coordinate0
    c. Undefined
    d. Undefined

Chapter 4. Systems of Equations and Inequalities

29. In mathematics, a _____ number is a number which can be expressed as a ratio of two integers. Non-integer _____ numbers (commonly called fractions) are usually written as the vulgar fraction a / b, where b is not zero.
    a. Thing
    b. Rational0
    c. Undefined
    d. Undefined

30. In mathematics, an _____ number is any real number that is not a rational number- that is, it is a number which cannot be expressed as a fraction m/n, where m and n are integers.
    a. Thing
    b. Irrational0
    c. Undefined
    d. Undefined

31. In mathematics, an _____ is any real number that is not a rational number ¡ª that is, it is a number which cannot be expressed as m/n, where m and n are integers.
    a. Irrational number0
    b. Thing
    c. Undefined
    d. Undefined

32. In mathematics, defined and _____ are used to explain whether or not expressions have meaningful, sensible, and unambiguous values.
    a. Thing
    b. Undefined0
    c. Undefined
    d. Undefined

33. In mathematics and its applications, a _____ is a system for assigning an n-tuple of numbers or scalars to each point in an n-dimensional space.
    a. Coordinate system0
    b. Concept
    c. Undefined
    d. Undefined

34. Equivalence is the condition of being _____ or essentially equal.
    a. Thing
    b. Equivalent0
    c. Undefined
    d. Undefined

35. _____ means of or relating to the French philosopher and mathematician RenÃ© Descartes.
    a. Cartesian0
    b. Thing
    c. Undefined
    d. Undefined

36. In mathematics, the _____ is used to determine each point uniquely in a plane through two numbers, usually called the x-coordinate and the y-coordinate of the point.
    a. Cartesian coordinate system0
    b. Thing
    c. Undefined
    d. Undefined

37. In geometry, two lines or planes if one falls on the other in such a way as to create congruent adjacent angles. The term may be used as a noun or adjective. Thus, referring to Figure 1, the line AB is the _____ to CD through the point B.
    a. Thing
    b. Perpendicular0
    c. Undefined
    d. Undefined

38. _____ is a set, with some particular properties and usually some additional structure, such as the operations of addition or multiplication, for instance.

Chapter 4. Systems of Equations and Inequalities

a. Thing
b. Space0
c. Undefined
d. Undefined

39. In mathematics, a _____ is a two-dimensional manifold or surface that is perfectly flat.
    a. Plane0
    b. Thing
    c. Undefined
    d. Undefined

40. The _____, the average in everyday English, which is also called the arithmetic _____ (and is distinguished from the geometric _____ or harmonic _____). The average is also called the sample _____. The expected value of a random variable, which is also called the population _____.
    a. Mean0
    b. Thing
    c. Undefined
    d. Undefined

41. In mathematics, _____ are two-dimensional manifolds or surfaces that are perfectly flat.
    a. Thing
    b. Planes0
    c. Undefined
    d. Undefined

42. In geometry, _____ lines are two lines that share one or more common points.
    a. Intersecting0
    b. Thing
    c. Undefined
    d. Undefined

43. _____ are a set of equations containing multiple variables.
    a. Thing
    b. Systems of equations0
    c. Undefined
    d. Undefined

44. In mathematics, a _____ is a polynomial equation of the second degree. The general form is $ax^2 + bx + c = 0$.
    a. Thing
    b. Quadratic equation0
    c. Undefined
    d. Undefined

45. A _____ is a unit of length, usually used to measure distance, in a number of different systems, including Imperial units, United States customary units and Norwegian/Swedish mil. Its size can vary from system to system, but in each is between 1 and 10 kilometers. In contemporary English contexts _____ refers to either:
    a. Thing
    b. Mile0
    c. Undefined
    d. Undefined

46. _____ is a unit of speed, expressing the number of international miles covered per hour.
    a. Thing
    b. Miles per hour0
    c. Undefined
    d. Undefined

47. _____ are a measure of time.
    a. Minutes0
    b. Thing
    c. Undefined
    d. Undefined

48. _____ is a way of expressing a number as a fraction of 100 per cent meaning "per hundred".

Chapter 4. Systems of Equations and Inequalities

    a. Thing
    c. Undefined
    b. Percent0
    d. Undefined

49. The plus and _____ signs are mathematical symbols used to represent the notions of positive and negative as well as the operations of addition and subtraction.
    a. Minus0
    c. Undefined
    b. Thing
    d. Undefined

50. _____ is a form of periodic payment from an employer to an employee, which is specified in an employment contract.
    a. Gross pay0
    c. Undefined
    b. Thing
    d. Undefined

51. The payment of _____ as remuneration for services rendered or products sold is a common way to reward sales people.
    a. Thing
    c. Undefined
    b. Commission0
    d. Undefined

52. A _____ is a form of periodic payment from an employer to an employee, which is specified in an employment contract.
    a. Thing
    c. Undefined
    b. Salary0
    d. Undefined

53. A _____ is a special kind of ratio, indicating a relationship between two measurements with different units, such as miles to gallons or cents to pounds.
    a. Thing
    c. Undefined
    b. Rate0
    d. Undefined

54. In botany, _____ are above-ground plant organs specialized for photosynthesis. Their characteristics are typically analyzed by using Fiobonacci's sequences.
    a. Thing
    c. Undefined
    b. Leaves0
    d. Undefined

55. The _____ of a solid object is the three-dimensional concept of how much space it occupies, often quantified numerically.
    a. Volume0
    c. Undefined
    b. Thing
    d. Undefined

56. _____ is a kind of property which exists as magnitude or multitude. It is among the basic classes of things along with quality, substance, change, and relation.
    a. Thing
    c. Undefined
    b. Amount0
    d. Undefined

57. In chemistry, a _____ is substance made by combining two or more different materials in such a way that no chemical reaction occurs.

Chapter 4. Systems of Equations and Inequalities

   a. Mixture0
   b. Thing
   c. Undefined
   d. Undefined

58. An _____ of a product of sums expresses it as a sum of products by using the fact that multiplication distributes over addition.
   a. Thing
   b. Expansion0
   c. Undefined
   d. Undefined

59. A _____ is a type of debt. All material things can be lent but this article focuses exclusively on monetary loans. Like all debt instruments, a _____ entails the redistribution of financial assets over time, between the lender and the borrower.
   a. Loan0
   b. Thing
   c. Undefined
   d. Undefined

60. _____ is the fee paid on borrowed money.
   a. Interest0
   b. Thing
   c. Undefined
   d. Undefined

61. In banking and accountancy, the outstanding _____ is the amount of money owned, or due, that remains in a deposit account or a loan account at a given date, after all past remittances, payments and withdrawal have been accounted for.
   a. Thing
   b. Balance0
   c. Undefined
   d. Undefined

62. An _____ is the fee paid on borrow money.
   a. Interest rate0
   b. Concept
   c. Undefined
   d. Undefined

63. _____ is the application of tools and a processing medium to the transformation of raw materials into finished goods for sale.
   a. Manufacturing0
   b. Thing
   c. Undefined
   d. Undefined

64. _____ is the ability to hold, receive or absorb, or a measure thereof, similar to the concept of volume.
   a. Concept
   b. Capacity0
   c. Undefined
   d. Undefined

65. A _____ given two distinct points A and B on the _____, is the set of points C on the line containing points A and B such that A is not strictly between C and B.
   a. Ray0
   b. Thing
   c. Undefined
   d. Undefined

66. In mathematical logic, a Gödel numbering (or Gödel _____) is a function that assigns to each symbol and well-formed formula of some formal language a unique natural number called its Gödel number.

a. Code0
b. Thing
c. Undefined
d. Undefined

67. In mathematics, computing, linguistics, and related disciplines, an _____ is a finite list of well-defined instructions for accomplishing some task which, given an initial state, will terminate in a defined end-state.
   a. Algorithm0
   b. Concept
   c. Undefined
   d. Undefined

68. A _____ is a deliberate process for transforming one or more inputs into one or more results.
   a. Thing
   b. Calculation0
   c. Undefined
   d. Undefined

69. The word _____ is used in a variety of ways in mathematics.
   a. Index0
   b. Thing
   c. Undefined
   d. Undefined

70. A _____ is a function that assigns a number to subsets of a given set.
   a. Thing
   b. Measure0
   c. Undefined
   d. Undefined

71. A pair of angles are _____ if the sum of their angles is 90°.
   a. Concept
   b. Complementary0
   c. Undefined
   d. Undefined

72. A pair of angles is _____ if their respective measures sum to 180 degrees.
   a. Concept
   b. Supplementary0
   c. Undefined
   d. Undefined

73. _____ is a state located in the southern and southwestern regions of the United States of America.
   a. Texas0
   b. Thing
   c. Undefined
   d. Undefined

74. In mathematics, a _____ function in the sense of algebraic geometry is an everywhere-defined, polynomial function on an algebraic variety V with values in the field K over which V is defined.
   a. Thing
   b. Regular0
   c. Undefined
   d. Undefined

75. A _____ are accounts maintained by commercial banks, savings and loan associations, credit unions, and mutual savings banks that pay interest but can not be used directly as money by, for example, writing a cheque.
   a. Savings account0
   b. Thing
   c. Undefined
   d. Undefined

76. _____ or investing is a term with several closely-related meanings in business management, finance and economics, related to saving or deferring consumption.

Chapter 4. Systems of Equations and Inequalities

a. Thing
b. Investment0
c. Undefined
d. Undefined

77. _____ is electromagnetic radiation with a wavelength that is visible to the eye (visible _____) or, in a technical or scientific context, electromagnetic radiation of any wavelength.
a. Thing
b. Light0
c. Undefined
d. Undefined

78. _____ is the transport of people on a trip/journey or the process or time involved in a person or object moving from one location to another.
a. Travel0
b. Thing
c. Undefined
d. Undefined

79. In mathematics, the additive inverse, or _____ of a number n is the number that, when added to n, yields zero. The additive inverse of n is denoted −n. For example, 7 is −7, because 7 + (−7) = 0, and the additive inverse of −0.3 is 0.3, because −0.3 + 0.3 = 0.
a. Thing
b. Opposite0
c. Undefined
d. Undefined

80. In mathematics, the _____ of a number n is the number that, when added to n, yields zero. The _____ of n is denoted −n. For example, 7 is −7, because 7 + (−7) = 0, and the _____ of −0.3 is 0.3, because −0.3 + 0.3 = 0.
a. Additive inverse0
b. Thing
c. Undefined
d. Undefined

81. Compass and straightedge or ruler-and-compass _____ is the _____ of lengths or angles using only an idealized ruler and compass.
a. Thing
b. Construction0
c. Undefined
d. Undefined

82. In the scientific method, an _____ (Latin: ex-+-periri, "of (or from) trying"), is a set of actions and observations, performed in the context of solving a particular problem or question, in order to support or falsify a hypothesis or research concerning phenomena.
a. Experiment0
b. Thing
c. Undefined
d. Undefined

83. In mathematics, there are several meanings of _____ depending on the subject.
a. Degree0
b. Thing
c. Undefined
d. Undefined

84. In geometry, the _____ of an object is a point in some sense in the middle of the object.
a. Center0
b. Thing
c. Undefined
d. Undefined

85. A _____ is one of the basic shapes of geometry: a polygon with three vertices and three sides which are straight line segments.

Chapter 4. Systems of Equations and Inequalities

    a. Triangle0
    b. Thing
    c. Undefined
    d. Undefined

86. _____ finance, in finance, a debt security, issued by Issuer
    a. Thing
    b. Bond0
    c. Undefined
    d. Undefined

87. _____, Greek for "knowledge of nature," is the branch of science concerned with the discovery and characterization of universal laws which govern matter, energy, space, and time.
    a. Physics0
    b. Thing
    c. Undefined
    d. Undefined

88. In physics, _____ is an influence that may cause an object to accelerate. It may be experienced as a lift, a push, or a pull. The actual acceleration of the body is determined by the vector sum of all forces acting on it, known as net _____ or resultant _____.
    a. Force0
    b. Thing
    c. Undefined
    d. Undefined

89. _____ systems represent systems whose behavior is not expressible as a sum of the behaviors of its descriptors.
    a. Thing
    b. Nonlinear0
    c. Undefined
    d. Undefined

90. A _____ represents a system whose behavior is not expressible as a sum of the behaviors of its descriptors.
    a. Thing
    b. Nonlinear system0
    c. Undefined
    d. Undefined

91. In mathematics, the concept of a _____ tries to capture the intuitive idea of a geometrical one-dimensional and continuous object. A simple example is the circle.
    a. Curve0
    b. Thing
    c. Undefined
    d. Undefined

92. In mathematics, _____ are the intuitive idea of a geometrical one-dimensional and continuous object.
    a. Curves0
    b. Thing
    c. Undefined
    d. Undefined

93. In linear algebra, the _____ of a matrix is obtained by combining two matrices in such a way that a matrix of coefficients to which has been added a column of constants corresponds to the right hand side of the equations.
    a. Augmented matrix0
    b. Thing
    c. Undefined
    d. Undefined

94. In mathematics, a _____ is a rectangular table of numbers or, more generally, a table consisting of abstract quantities that can be added and multiplied.
    a. Thing
    b. Matrix0
    c. Undefined
    d. Undefined

Chapter 4. Systems of Equations and Inequalities

95. In computer science an _____ is a data structure that consists of a group of elements having a single name that are accessed by indexing. In most programming languages each element has the same data type and the _____ occupies a continuous area of storage.
    a. Thing
    b. Array0
    c. Undefined
    d. Undefined

96. The _____ (symbol _____) and the millibar (symbol mbar, also mb) are units of pressure.
    a. Bar0
    b. Thing
    c. Undefined
    d. Undefined

97. _____ is a special kind of square matrix where the entries below or above the main diagonal are zero.
    a. Triangular form0
    b. Thing
    c. Undefined
    d. Undefined

98. In mathematics, a _____ in elementary terms is any of a variety of different functions from geometry, such as rotations, reflections and translations.
    a. Thing
    b. Transformation0
    c. Undefined
    d. Undefined

99. In mathematics, a _____ may be described informally as a number that can be given by an infinite decimal representation.
    a. Thing
    b. Real number0
    c. Undefined
    d. Undefined

100. An _____ or member of a set is an object that when collected together make up the set.
    a. Element0
    b. Thing
    c. Undefined
    d. Undefined

101. In mathematics, a matrix can be thought of as each row or _____ being a vector. Hence, a space formed by row vectors or _____ vectors are said to be a row space or a _____ space.
    a. Concept
    b. Column0
    c. Undefined
    d. Undefined

102. In mathematics, _____ is an elementary arithmetic operation. When one of the numbers is a whole number, _____ is the repeated sum of the other number.
    a. Thing
    b. Multiplication0
    c. Undefined
    d. Undefined

103. In mathematics, a _____ is the result of multiplying, or an expression that identifies factors to be multiplied.
    a. Product0
    b. Thing
    c. Undefined
    d. Undefined

104. In geometry, a _____ is the intersection of a body in 2-dimensional space with a line, or of a body in 3-dimensional space with a plane

Chapter 4. Systems of Equations and Inequalities

   a. Thing
   b. Cross section0
   c. Undefined
   d. Undefined

105. In mathematics, an inequality is a statement about the relative size or order of two objects. For example 14 > 10, or 14 is _____ 10.
   a. Greater than0
   b. Thing
   c. Undefined
   d. Undefined

106. In geometry and trigonometry, a _____ is defined as an angle between two straight intersecting lines of ninety degrees, or one-quarter of a circle.
   a. Right angle0
   b. Thing
   c. Undefined
   d. Undefined

107. The population _____ is the total number of human beings alive on the planet Earth at a given time.
   a. Of the world0
   b. Thing
   c. Undefined
   d. Undefined

108. A circular _____ or circle _____ also known as a pie piece is the portion of a circle enclosed by two radii and an arc.
   a. Thing
   b. Sector0
   c. Undefined
   d. Undefined

109. In Euclidean geometry, a _____ is the set of all points in a plane at a fixed distance, called the radius, from a given point, the center.
   a. Circle0
   b. Thing
   c. Undefined
   d. Undefined

110. In algebra, a _____ is a function depending on n that associates a scalar, det(A), to every $n \times n$ square matrix A.
   a. Determinant0
   b. Thing
   c. Undefined
   d. Undefined

111. In plane geometry, a _____ is a polygon with four equal sides, four right angles, and parallel opposite sides. In algebra, the _____ of a number is that number multiplied by itself.
   a. Thing
   b. Square0
   c. Undefined
   d. Undefined

112. Mathematical _____ is used to represent ideas.
   a. Thing
   b. Notation0
   c. Undefined
   d. Undefined

113. A _____ is a numeral used to indicate a count. The most common use of the word today is to name the part of a fraction that tells the number or count of equal parts.
   a. Thing
   b. Numerator0
   c. Undefined
   d. Undefined

Chapter 4. Systems of Equations and Inequalities

114. A _____ is a number, figure, or indicator that appears below the normal line of type, typically used in a formula, mathematical expression, or description of a chemical compound.
 a. Thing
 b. Subscript0
 c. Undefined
 d. Undefined

115. In mathematics, the _____ , or members of a set or more generally a class are all those objects which when collected together make up the set or class.
 a. Thing
 b. Elements0
 c. Undefined
 d. Undefined

116. In linear algebra, a _____ of a matrix A is the determinant of some smaller square matrix, cut down from A.
 a. Minor0
 b. Thing
 c. Undefined
 d. Undefined

117. In mathematics, an _____ is a statement about the relative size or order of two objects.
 a. Inequality0
 b. Thing
 c. Undefined
 d. Undefined

118. In mathematics, the _____ (or modulus) of a real number is its numerical value without regard to its sign.
 a. Absolute value0
 b. Thing
 c. Undefined
 d. Undefined

119. In mathematics, _____ geometry was the traditional name for the geometry of three-dimensional Euclidean space — for practical purposes the kind of space we live in.
 a. Solid0
 b. Thing
 c. Undefined
 d. Undefined

120. A _____ consists of one quarter of the coordinate plane.
 a. Thing
 b. Quadrant0
 c. Undefined
 d. Undefined

121. In mathematics, the _____ of a function is the set of all "output" values produced by that function. Given a function $f : A \rightarrow B$, the _____ of f, is defined to be the set $\{x \in B : x = f(a)$ for some $a \in A\}$.
 a. Range0
 b. Thing
 c. Undefined
 d. Undefined

122. In mathematics, a _____ of a k-place relation $L \subseteq X_1 \times ... \times X_k$ is one of the sets X_j, $1 \leq j \leq k$. In the special case where k = 2 and $L \subseteq X_1 \times X_2$ is a function $L : X_1 \rightarrow X_2$, it is conventional to refer to X_1 as the _____ of the function and to refer to X_2 as the codomain of the function.
 a. Thing
 b. Domain0
 c. Undefined
 d. Undefined

123. Acid _____ ratio measures the ability of a company to use its near cash or quick assets to immediately extinguish its current liabilities.

a. Thing
b. Test0
c. Undefined
d. Undefined

124. In mathematics, a _____ can mean either an element of the set {1, 2, 3, ...} (i.e the positive integers or the counting numbers) or an element of the set {0, 1, 2, 3, ...} (i.e. the non-negative integers).
   a. Natural number0
   b. Thing
   c. Undefined
   d. Undefined

125. In mathematics, a _____ is a number which can be expressed as a ratio of two integers. Non-integer rational numbers (commonly called fractions) are usually written as the vulgar fraction a / b, where b is not zero.
   a. Rational Number0
   b. Concept
   c. Undefined
   d. Undefined

126. A _____ is a set of possible values that a variable can take on in order to satisfy a given set of conditions, which may include equations and inequalities.
   a. Thing
   b. Solution set0
   c. Undefined
   d. Undefined

127. A _____ is an abstract model that uses mathematical language to describe the behavior of a system. Eykhoff defined a _____ as 'a representation of the essential aspects of an existing system which presents knowledge of that system in usable form'.
   a. Mathematical model0
   b. Thing
   c. Undefined
   d. Undefined

128. _____ is a business term for the amount of money that a company receives from its activities in a given period, mostly from sales of products and/or services to customers
   a. Revenue0
   b. Thing
   c. Undefined
   d. Undefined

Chapter 5. Polynomials and Polynomial Functions

1. In mathematics, a _____ is an expression that is constructed from one or more variables and constants, using only the operations of addition, subtraction, multiplication, and constant positive whole number exponents. is a _____. Note in particular that division by an expression containing a variable is not in general allowed in polynomials. [1]
   - a. Polynomial0
   - b. Thing
   - c. Undefined
   - d. Undefined

2. The mathematical concept of a _____ expresses the intuitive idea of deterministic dependence between two quantities, one of which is viewed as primary and the other as secondary. A _____ then is a way to associate a unique output for each input of a specified type, for example, a real number or an element of a given set.
   - a. Function0
   - b. Thing
   - c. Undefined
   - d. Undefined

3. _____ are the basic objects of study in graph theory. Informally speaking, a graph is a set of objects called points, nodes, or vertices connected by links called lines or edges.
   - a. Graphs0
   - b. Thing
   - c. Undefined
   - d. Undefined

4. A _____ is 360° or 2∂ radians.
   - a. Turn0
   - b. Thing
   - c. Undefined
   - d. Undefined

5. In mathematics, _____ is the decomposition of an object into a product of other objects, or factors, which when multiplied together give the original.
   - a. Factoring0
   - b. Thing
   - c. Undefined
   - d. Undefined

6. A _____ is a polynomial function of the form $f(x) = ax^2 + bx + c$, where a, b, c are real numbers and a , 0.
   - a. Event
   - b. Quadratic function0
   - c. Undefined
   - d. Undefined

7. In geometry, the _____ of an object is a point in some sense in the middle of the object.
   - a. Thing
   - b. Center0
   - c. Undefined
   - d. Undefined

8. An _____ is a combination of numbers, operators, grouping symbols and/or free variables and bound variables arranged in a meaningful way which can be evaluated..
   - a. Thing
   - b. Expression0
   - c. Undefined
   - d. Undefined

9. In mathematics, there are several meanings of _____ depending on the subject.
   - a. Thing
   - b. Degree0
   - c. Undefined
   - d. Undefined

10. The _____ is the maximum of the degrees of all terms in the polynomial.
    - a. Thing
    - b. Degree of a polynomial0
    - c. Undefined
    - d. Undefined

Chapter 5. Polynomials and Polynomial Functions

11. A _____ is a symbolic representation denoting a quantity or expression. It often represents an "unknown" quantity that has the potential to change.
    a. Variable0
    b. Thing
    c. Undefined
    d. Undefined

12. A _____ is the result of the addition of a set of numbers. The numbers may be natural numbers, complex numbers, matrices, or still more complicated objects. An infinite _____ is a subtle procedure known as a series.
    a. Thing
    b. Sum0
    c. Undefined
    d. Undefined

13. In mathematics, a _____ can mean either an element of the set {1, 2, 3, ...} (i.e the positive integers) or an element of the set {0, 1, 2, 3, ...} (i.e. the non-negative integers).
    a. Whole number0
    b. Concept
    c. Undefined
    d. Undefined

14. _____ is a mathematical operation, written a^n, involving two numbers, the base a and the exponent n.
    a. Thing
    b. Exponentiating0
    c. Undefined
    d. Undefined

15. _____ is a mathematical operation, written a^n, involving two numbers, the base a and the exponent n.
    a. Exponentiation0
    b. Thing
    c. Undefined
    d. Undefined

16. The _____ is the sum of the exponents of the variables in the term.
    a. Thing
    b. Degree of a term0
    c. Undefined
    d. Undefined

17. In mathematics and the mathematical sciences, a _____ is a fixed, but possibly unspecified, value. This is in contrast to a variable, which is not fixed.
    a. Thing
    b. Constant0
    c. Undefined
    d. Undefined

18. A _____ is the part of a fraction that tells how many equal parts make up a whole, and which is used in the name of the fraction: "halves", "thirds", "fourths" or "quarters", "fifths" and so on.
    a. Denominator0
    b. Concept
    c. Undefined
    d. Undefined

19. In mathematics, a set is called _____ if there is a bijection between the set and some set of the form {1, 2, ..., n} where n is a natural number.
    a. Finite0
    b. Thing
    c. Undefined
    d. Undefined

20. In mathematics, a _____ is a constant multiplicative factor of a certain object. The object can be such things as a variable, a vector, a function, etc. For example, the _____ of $9x^2$ is 9.

Chapter 5. Polynomials and Polynomial Functions

a. Coefficient0
b. Thing
c. Undefined
d. Undefined

21. _____, from Latin meaning "to make progress", is defined in two different ways. Pure economic _____ is the increase in wealth that an investor has from making an investment, taking into consideration all costs associated with that investment including the opportunity cost of capital.
 a. Thing
 b. Profit0
 c. Undefined
 d. Undefined

22. In mathematics, a _____ is any one of several different types of functions, mappings, operations, or transformations.
 a. Thing
 b. Projection0
 c. Undefined
 d. Undefined

23. In sociology and biology a _____ is the collection of people or organisms of a particular species living in a given geographic area or space, usually measured by a census.
 a. Population0
 b. Thing
 c. Undefined
 d. Undefined

24. _____ is a business term for the amount of money that a company receives from its activities in a given period, mostly from sales of products and/or services to customers
 a. Thing
 b. Revenue0
 c. Undefined
 d. Undefined

25. _____ is the transport of people on a trip/journey or the process or time involved in a person or object moving from one location to another.
 a. Thing
 b. Travel0
 c. Undefined
 d. Undefined

26. A _____ is a negotiable instrument instructing a financial institution to pay a specific amount of a specific currency from a specific demand account held in the maker/depositor's name with that institution. Both the maker and payee may be natural persons or legal entities.
 a. Thing
 b. Check0
 c. Undefined
 d. Undefined

27. In mathematics, the concept of a _____ tries to capture the intuitive idea of a geometrical one-dimensional and continuous object. A simple example is the circle.
 a. Thing
 b. Curve0
 c. Undefined
 d. Undefined

28. In mathematics, the _____ of a function is the set of all "output" values produced by that function. Given a function $f : A \rightarrow B$, the _____ of f, is defined to be the set $\{x \in B : x = f(a) \text{ for some } a \in A\}$.
 a. Thing
 b. Range0
 c. Undefined
 d. Undefined

29. _____, either of the curved-bracket punctuation marks that together make a set of _____

Chapter 5. Polynomials and Polynomial Functions

   a. Thing   b. Parentheses0
   c. Undefined   d. Undefined

30. A _____ is a polygon with four sides and four vertices.
   a. Quadrilateral0   b. Thing
   c. Undefined   d. Undefined

31. _____ is the distance around a given two-dimensional object. As a general rule, the _____ of a polygon can always be calculated by adding all the length of the sides together. So, the formula for triangles is P = a + b + c, where a, b and c stand for each side of it. For quadrilaterals the equation is P = a + b + c + d. For equilateral polygons, P = na, where n is the number of sides and a is the side length.
   a. Perimeter0   b. Thing
   c. Undefined   d. Undefined

32. In business, particularly accounting, a _____ is the time intervals that the accounts, statement, payments, or other calculations cover.
   a. Thing   b. Period0
   c. Undefined   d. Undefined

33. In banking and accountancy, the outstanding _____ is the amount of money owned, or due, that remains in a deposit account or a loan account at a given date, after all past remittances, payments and withdrawal have been accounted for.
   a. Balance0   b. Thing
   c. Undefined   d. Undefined

34. The _____ (symbol _____) and the millibar (symbol mbar, also mb) are units of pressure.
   a. Bar0   b. Thing
   c. Undefined   d. Undefined

35. _____ (Groups, Algorithms and Programming) is a computer algebra system for computational discrete algebra with particular emphasis on, but not restricted to, computational group theory.
   a. Gap0   b. Thing
   c. Undefined   d. Undefined

36. A _____ is a number that is less than zero.
   a. Negative number0   b. Thing
   c. Undefined   d. Undefined

37. The plus and _____ signs are mathematical symbols used to represent the notions of positive and negative as well as the operations of addition and subtraction.
   a. Minus0   b. Thing
   c. Undefined   d. Undefined

38. A _____ is a polynomial consisting of three terms; in other words, it is the sum of three monomials.

Chapter 5. Polynomials and Polynomial Functions 69

  a. Thing
  b. Trinomial0
  c. Undefined
  d. Undefined

39. The _____, the average in everyday English, which is also called the arithmetic _____ (and is distinguished from the geometric _____ or harmonic _____). The average is also called the sample _____. The expected value of a random variable, which is also called the population _____.
  a. Thing
  b. Mean0
  c. Undefined
  d. Undefined

40. In mathematics, a _____ is a particular kind of polynomial, having just one term.
  a. Monomial0
  b. Thing
  c. Undefined
  d. Undefined

41. In elementary algebra, a _____ is a polynomial with two terms: the sum of two monomials. It is the simplest kind of polynomial except for a monomial.
  a. Binomial0
  b. Thing
  c. Undefined
  d. Undefined

42. In mathematics, a _____ can mean either an element of the set {1, 2, 3, ...} (i.e the positive integers or the counting numbers) or an element of the set {0, 1, 2, 3, ...} (i.e. the non-negative integers).
  a. Thing
  b. Natural number0
  c. Undefined
  d. Undefined

43. _____ forms part of thinking. Considered the most complex of all intellectual functions, _____ has been defined as higher-order cognitive process that requires the modulation and control of more routine or fundamental skills.
  a. Problem solving0
  b. Thing
  c. Undefined
  d. Undefined

44. In Euclidean geometry, a _____ is the set of all points in a plane at a fixed distance, called the radius, from a given point, the center.
  a. Circle0
  b. Thing
  c. Undefined
  d. Undefined

45. In classical geometry, a _____ of a circle or sphere is any line segment from its center to its boundary. By extension, the _____ of a circle or sphere is the length of any such segment. The _____ is half the diameter. In science and engineering the term _____ of curvature is commonly used as a synonym for _____.
  a. Thing
  b. Radius0
  c. Undefined
  d. Undefined

46. The _____ of a solid object is the three-dimensional concept of how much space it occupies, often quantified numerically.
  a. Thing
  b. Volume0
  c. Undefined
  d. Undefined

Chapter 5. Polynomials and Polynomial Functions

47. In mathematics, a _____ is the set of all points in three-dimensional space (R^3) which are at distance r from a fixed point of that space, where r is a positive real number called the radius of the _____. The fixed point is called the center or centre, and is not part of the _____ itself.
 a. Thing
 b. Sphere0
 c. Undefined
 d. Undefined

48. A bar chart, also known as a _____, is a chart with rectangular bars of lengths usually proportional to the magnitudes or frequencies of what they represent.
 a. Thing
 b. Bar graph0
 c. Undefined
 d. Undefined

49. The _____ is one of the classical simple machines; as the name suggests, it is a flat surface whose endpoints are at different heights. By moving an object up an _____ rather than directly from one height to another, the amount of force required is reduced, at the expense of increasing the distance the object must travel. The mechanical advantage of an _____ is the ratio of the length of the sloped surface to the height it spans; this may also be expressed as the cosecant of the angle between the plane and the horizontal.
 a. Inclined plane0
 b. Thing
 c. Undefined
 d. Undefined

50. In mathematics, a _____ is a two-dimensional manifold or surface that is perfectly flat.
 a. Plane0
 b. Thing
 c. Undefined
 d. Undefined

51. In mainstream economics, the word _____ refers to a general rise in prices measured against a standard level of purchasing power.
 a. Thing
 b. Inflation0
 c. Undefined
 d. Undefined

52. _____ has many meanings, most of which simply .
 a. Power0
 b. Thing
 c. Undefined
 d. Undefined

53. A _____ is a special kind of ratio, indicating a relationship between two measurements with different units, such as miles to gallons or cents to pounds.
 a. Thing
 b. Rate0
 c. Undefined
 d. Undefined

54. _____ is a way of expressing a number as a fraction of 100 per cent meaning "per hundred".
 a. Percent0
 b. Thing
 c. Undefined
 d. Undefined

55. In mathematics, an inequality is a statement about the relative size or order of two objects. For example 14 > 10, or 14 is _____ 10.
 a. Greater than0
 b. Thing
 c. Undefined
 d. Undefined

Chapter 5. Polynomials and Polynomial Functions

56. In mathematics, a _____ may be described informally as a number that can be given by an infinite decimal representation.
   a. Real number0
   b. Thing
   c. Undefined
   d. Undefined

57. In mathematics, _____ is an elementary arithmetic operation. When one of the numbers is a whole number, _____ is the repeated sum of the other number.
   a. Multiplication0
   b. Thing
   c. Undefined
   d. Undefined

58. _____ is often used to describe the measurement of the steepness, incline, gradient, or grade of a straight line. The _____ is defined as the ratio of the "rise" divided by the "run" between two points on a line, or in other words, the ratio of the altitude change to the horizontal distance between any two points on the line.
   a. Slope0
   b. Thing
   c. Undefined
   d. Undefined

59. In mathematics, a _____ is the result of multiplying, or an expression that identifies factors to be multiplied.
   a. Thing
   b. Product0
   c. Undefined
   d. Undefined

60. In plane geometry, a _____ is a polygon with four equal sides, four right angles, and parallel opposite sides. In algebra, the _____ of a number is that number multiplied by itself.
   a. Square0
   b. Thing
   c. Undefined
   d. Undefined

61. The _____ governs the differentiation of products of differentiable functions.
   a. Thing
   b. Product rule0
   c. Undefined
   d. Undefined

62. In mathematics, a _____ is the end result of a division problem. It can also be expressed as the number of times the divisor divides into the dividend.
   a. Thing
   b. Quotient0
   c. Undefined
   d. Undefined

63. The _____ is a method of finding the derivative of a function that is the quotient of two other functions for which derivatives exist.
   a. Thing
   b. Quotient rule0
   c. Undefined
   d. Undefined

64. In mathematics, factorization (British English: factorisation) or factoring is the decomposition of an object (for example, a number, a polynomial, or a matrix) into a product of other objects, or _____, which when multiplied together give the original.
   a. Factors0
   b. Thing
   c. Undefined
   d. Undefined

65. The _____ of an algebraic expression is the same equation, but without parentheses.

Chapter 5. Polynomials and Polynomial Functions

    a. Thing
    b. Expanded form0
    c. Undefined
    d. Undefined

66. In mathematics, and in particular in abstract algebra, the _____ is a property of binary operations that generalises the distributive law from elementary algebra.
    a. Distributive property0
    b. Thing
    c. Undefined
    d. Undefined

67. In mathematics, a matrix can be thought of as each row or _____ being a vector. Hence, a space formed by row vectors or _____ vectors are said to be a row space or a _____ space.
    a. Concept
    b. Column0
    c. Undefined
    d. Undefined

68. _____ also sometimes known as the double distributive property or more colloquially as foiling, is commonly taught to US high school students learning algebra as a mnemonic for remembering how to multiply two binomials polynomials with two terms.
    a. FOIL method0
    b. Thing
    c. Undefined
    d. Undefined

69. The _____ is commonly taught to US high school students learning algebra as a mnemonic for remembering how to multiply two binomials.
    a. FOIL rule0
    b. Thing
    c. Undefined
    d. Undefined

70. In geometry, a _____ is defined as a quadrilateral where all four of its angles are right angles.
    a. Rectangle0
    b. Thing
    c. Undefined
    d. Undefined

71. _____ is the fee paid on borrowed money.
    a. Thing
    b. Interest0
    c. Undefined
    d. Undefined

72. In mathematics, _____ allows the rapid division of any polynomial by a binomial of the form x − r. It was described by Paolo Ruffini in 1809. _____ is a special case of long division when the divisor is a linear factor.
    a. Thing
    b. Ruffini's rule0
    c. Undefined
    d. Undefined

73. _____ interest refers to the fact that whenever interest is calculated, it is based not only on the original principal, but also on any unpaid interest that has been added to the principal.
    a. Thing
    b. Compound0
    c. Undefined
    d. Undefined

74. _____ refers to the fact that whenever interest is calculated, it is based not only on the original principal, but also on any unpaid interest that has been added to the principal. The more frequently interest is compounded, the faster the balance grows.

Chapter 5. Polynomials and Polynomial Functions

a. Compound interest0
b. Concept
c. Undefined
d. Undefined

75. _____ is a kind of property which exists as magnitude or multitude. It is among the basic classes of things along with quality, substance, change, and relation.
    a. Amount0
    b. Thing
    c. Undefined
    d. Undefined

76. Mathematical _____ is used to represent ideas.
    a. Thing
    b. Notation0
    c. Undefined
    d. Undefined

77. In mathematics, an _____ is a statement about the relative size or order of two objects.
    a. Thing
    b. Inequality0
    c. Undefined
    d. Undefined

78. In elementary algebra, an _____ is a set that contains every real number between two indicated numbers and may contain the two numbers themselves.
    a. Interval0
    b. Thing
    c. Undefined
    d. Undefined

79. _____ is the notation in which permitted values for a variable are expressed as ranging over a certain interval; "5 < x < 9" is an example of the application of _____.
    a. Thing
    b. Interval notation0
    c. Undefined
    d. Undefined

80. In arithmetic, _____ is a procedure for calculating the division of one integer, called the dividend, by another integer called the divisor, to produce a result called the quotient.
    a. Thing
    b. Long division0
    c. Undefined
    d. Undefined

81. _____ is a payment made by a company to its shareholders
    a. Dividend0
    b. Thing
    c. Undefined
    d. Undefined

82. In mathematics, a _____ of an integer n, also called a factor of n, is an integer which evenly divides n without leaving a remainder.
    a. Divisor0
    b. Thing
    c. Undefined
    d. Undefined

83. A _____ is the part of the dividend that is left over when the dividend is not evenly divisible by the divisor.
    a. Thing
    b. Remainder0
    c. Undefined
    d. Undefined

84. _____ the expected value of a random variable displays the average or central value of the variable. It is a summary value of the distribution of the variable.

Chapter 5. Polynomials and Polynomial Functions

    a. Determining0   b. Thing
    c. Undefined   d. Undefined

85. The deductive-nomological model is a formalized view of scientific _____ in natural language.
    a. Explanation0   b. Thing
    c. Undefined   d. Undefined

86. _____ is a set, with some particular properties and usually some additional structure, such as the operations of addition or multiplication, for instance.
    a. Thing   b. Space0
    c. Undefined   d. Undefined

87. In astronomy, geography, geometry and related sciences and contexts, a plane is said to be _____ at a given point if it is locally perpendicular to the gradient of the gravity field, i.e., with the direction of the gravitational force at that point.
    a. Horizontal0   b. Thing
    c. Undefined   d. Undefined

88. _____ in algebra is an application of polynomial long division.
    a. Thing   b. Remainder theorem0
    c. Undefined   d. Undefined

89. In mathematics, a _____ is a statement that can be proved on the basis of explicitly stated or previously agreed assumptions.
    a. Theorem0   b. Thing
    c. Undefined   d. Undefined

90. _____ is a notation for writing numbers that is often used by scientists and mathematicians to make it easier to write large and small numbers.
    a. Thing   b. Scientific notation0
    c. Undefined   d. Undefined

91. A _____ is one of the basic shapes of geometry: a polygon with three vertices and three sides which are straight line segments.
    a. Thing   b. Triangle0
    c. Undefined   d. Undefined

92. A _____ is a numeral used to indicate a count. The most common use of the word today is to name the part of a fraction that tells the number or count of equal parts.
    a. Numerator0   b. Thing
    c. Undefined   d. Undefined

93. In mathematics, the _____ divisor of two non-zero integers, is the largest positive integer that divides both numbers without remainder.
    a. Thing   b. Greatest common0
    c. Undefined   d. Undefined

Chapter 5. Polynomials and Polynomial Functions

94. In Math the greates common divisor sometimes known as the _____ of two non- zero integers.
    a. Thing
    b. Greatest common factor0
    c. Undefined
    d. Undefined

95. A _____ is a set of possible values that a variable can take on in order to satisfy a given set of conditions, which may include equations and inequalities.
    a. Solution set0
    b. Thing
    c. Undefined
    d. Undefined

96. _____ is the largest positive integer that divides both numbers without remainder.
    a. Common Factor0
    b. Thing
    c. Undefined
    d. Undefined

97. In mathematics, the additive inverse, or _____ of a number n is the number that, when added to n, yields zero. The additive inverse of n is denoted −n. For example, 7 is −7, because 7 + (−7) = 0, and the additive inverse of −0.3 is 0.3, because −0.3 + 0.3 = 0.
    a. Thing
    b. Opposite0
    c. Undefined
    d. Undefined

98. In mathematics, the _____ of a number n is the number that, when added to n, yields zero. The _____ of n is denoted −n. For example, 7 is −7, because 7 + (−7) = 0, and the _____ of −0.3 is 0.3, because −0.3 + 0.3 = 0.
    a. Thing
    b. Additive inverse0
    c. Undefined
    d. Undefined

99. _____ of an object is its speed in a particular direction.
    a. Thing
    b. Velocity0
    c. Undefined
    d. Undefined

100. The _____ is a property of multiplication or addition where the product or sum remains the same, regardless of whether or not the order of the addends or factors are changed.
    a. Thing
    b. Commutative property0
    c. Undefined
    d. Undefined

101. Equivalence is the condition of being _____ or essentially equal.
    a. Thing
    b. Equivalent0
    c. Undefined
    d. Undefined

102. In abstract algebra, _____ consists of sets with binary operations that satisfy certain axioms.
    a. Grouping0
    b. Thing
    c. Undefined
    d. Undefined

103. A _____ is a quadrilateral, which is defined as a shape with four sides, which has a pair of parallel sides.
    a. Trapezoid0
    b. Thing
    c. Undefined
    d. Undefined

104. _____ of a product is the price the manufacturer recommends that the retailer sell it for.

Chapter 5. Polynomials and Polynomial Functions

    a. Thing   b. List price0
    c. Undefined   d. Undefined

105. In mathematics, a _____ function in the sense of algebraic geometry is an everywhere-defined, polynomial function on an algebraic variety V with values in the field K over which V is defined.
    a. Regular0   b. Thing
    c. Undefined   d. Undefined

106. The _____ are the only integral domain whose positive elements are well-ordered, and in which order is preserved by addition. Like the natural numbers, the _____ form a countably infinite set. The set of all _____ is usually denoted in mathematics by a boldface Z .
    a. Thing   b. Integers0
    c. Undefined   d. Undefined

107. _____ are any documents that aim to streamline particular processes according to a set routine.
    a. Thing   b. Guidelines0
    c. Undefined   d. Undefined

108. In mathematics, the conjugate _____ or adjoint matrix of an m-by-n matrix A with complex entries is the n-by-m matrix A* obtained from A by taking the transpose and then taking the complex conjugate of each entry.
    a. Thing   b. Pairs0
    c. Undefined   d. Undefined

109. In combinatorial mathematics, a _____ is an un-ordered collection of unique elements.
    a. Combination0   b. Concept
    c. Undefined   d. Undefined

110. _____ is a fixed, but possibly unspecified, value. This is in contrast to a variable, which is not fixed.
    a. Constant term0   b. Thing
    c. Undefined   d. Undefined

111. In mathematics, a _____ number (or a _____) is a natural number that has exactly two (distinct) natural number divisors, which are 1 and the _____ number itself.
    a. Prime0   b. Thing
    c. Undefined   d. Undefined

112. The term _____ can refer to an integer which is the square of some other integer, or an algebraic expression that can be factored as the square of some other expression.
    a. Perfect square0   b. Thing
    c. Undefined   d. Undefined

113. In mathematics, a _____ of a number x is a number r such that $r^2 = x$, or in words, a number r whose square (the result of multiplying the number by itself) is x.
    a. Thing   b. Square root0
    c. Undefined   d. Undefined

Chapter 5. Polynomials and Polynomial Functions

114. In mathematics, a _____ of a complex-valued function f is a member x of the domain of f such that f(x) vanishes at x, that is, x : f (x) = 0.
 a. Root0
 b. Thing
 c. Undefined
 d. Undefined

115. In algebra, a _____ is a function depending on *n* that associates a scalar, det(*A*), to every *n×n* square matrix *A*.
 a. Thing
 b. Determinant0
 c. Undefined
 d. Undefined

116. In mathematics the _____ refers to the identity: $a^2 - b^2 = (a+b)(a-b)$
 a. Thing
 b. Difference of two squares0
 c. Undefined
 d. Undefined

117. A _____ is a three-dimensional solid object bounded by six square faces, facets, or sides, with three meeting at each vertex.
 a. Thing
 b. Cube0
 c. Undefined
 d. Undefined

118. _____ are of a number n in its third power-the result of multiplying it by itself three times.
 a. Cubes0
 b. Thing
 c. Undefined
 d. Undefined

119. The word _____ comes from the Latin word linearis, which means created by lines.
 a. Linear0
 b. Thing
 c. Undefined
 d. Undefined

120. In geometry and trigonometry, a _____ is defined as an angle between two straight intersecting lines of ninety degrees, or one-quarter of a circle.
 a. Right angle0
 b. Thing
 c. Undefined
 d. Undefined

121. In mathematics, a _____ is a polynomial equation of the second degree. The general form is $ax^2 + bx + c = 0$.
 a. Thing
 b. Quadratic equation0
 c. Undefined
 d. Undefined

122. In a right triangle, the _____ of the triangle are the two sides that are perpendicular to each other, as opposed to the hypotenuse.
 a. Thing
 b. Legs0
 c. Undefined
 d. Undefined

123. The _____ of a right triangle is the triangle's longest side; the side opposite the right angle.
 a. Hypotenuse0
 b. Thing
 c. Undefined
 d. Undefined

124. _____ has one 90° internal angle a right angle.

Chapter 5. Polynomials and Polynomial Functions

a. Thing
b. Right triangle0
c. Undefined
d. Undefined

125. _____ is a relation in Euclidean geometry among the three sides of a right triangle.
a. Thing
b. Pythagorean Theorem0
c. Undefined
d. Undefined

126. In linear algebra, the _____ of an n-by-n square matrix A is defined to be the sum of the elements on the main diagonal of A,
a. Thing
b. Trace0
c. Undefined
d. Undefined

127. Any point where a graph makes contact with an coordinate axis is called an _____ of the graph
a. Thing
b. Intercept0
c. Undefined
d. Undefined

128. Regrouping is the act of putting ones into groups of 10. For example, the 1 on the far right of 131 would be denoted _____ if the digit of the number being subtracted is larger than 1, such as 131-99.
a. By 100
b. Thing
c. Undefined
d. Undefined

129. A _____ is any object propelled through space by the applicationp of a force.
a. Projectile0
b. Thing
c. Undefined
d. Undefined

130. A _____ is a vehicle, missile or aircraft which obtains thrust by the reaction to the ejection of fast moving fluid from within a _____ engine.
a. Rocket0
b. Thing
c. Undefined
d. Undefined

131. A _____ is a unit of length, usually used to measure distance, in a number of different systems, including Imperial units, United States customary units and Norwegian/Swedish mil. Its size can vary from system to system, but in each is between 1 and 10 kilometers. In contemporary English contexts _____ refers to either:
a. Mile0
b. Thing
c. Undefined
d. Undefined

132. _____ is a unit of speed, expressing the number of international miles covered per hour.
a. Thing
b. Miles per hour0
c. Undefined
d. Undefined

133. _____ is the state of being greater than any finite real or natural number, however large.
a. Thing
b. Infinite0
c. Undefined
d. Undefined

134. A _____ is a one-dimensional picture in which the integers are shown as specially-marked points evenly spaced on a line.

Chapter 5. Polynomials and Polynomial Functions

a. Number line0
b. Thing
c. Undefined
d. Undefined

135. _____ primarily refers to social welfare service concerned with social protection, or protection against socially recognized conditions, including poverty, old age, disability, unemployment, families with children and others.
   a. Social security0
   b. Thing
   c. Undefined
   d. Undefined

136. The metre (or _____, see spelling differences) is a measure of length. It is the basic unit of length in the metric system and in the International System of Units (SI), used around the world for general and scientific purposes.
   a. Concept
   b. Meter0
   c. Undefined
   d. Undefined

137. Initial objects are also called _____, and terminal objects are also called final.
   a. Thing
   b. Coterminal0
   c. Undefined
   d. Undefined

138. Acid _____ ratio measures the ability of a company to use its near cash or quick assets to immediately extinguish its current liabilities.
   a. Test0
   b. Thing
   c. Undefined
   d. Undefined

Chapter 6. Rational Expressions and Equations

1. In mathematics, a _____ number is a number which can be expressed as a ratio of two integers. Non-integer _____ numbers (commonly called fractions) are usually written as the vulgar fraction a / b, where b is not zero.
    a. Rational0
    b. Thing
    c. Undefined
    d. Undefined

2. An _____ is a combination of numbers, operators, grouping symbols and/or free variables and bound variables arranged in a meaningful way which can be evaluated..
    a. Expression0
    b. Thing
    c. Undefined
    d. Undefined

3. In mathematics, a _____ is any function which can be written as the ratio of two polynomial functions.
    a. Rational function0
    b. Thing
    c. Undefined
    d. Undefined

4. The mathematical concept of a _____ expresses the intuitive idea of deterministic dependence between two quantities, one of which is viewed as primary and the other as secondary. A _____ then is a way to associate a unique output for each input of a specified type, for example, a real number or an element of a given set.
    a. Function0
    b. Thing
    c. Undefined
    d. Undefined

5. In mathematics, a _____ of a k-place relation $L \subseteq X_1 \times ... \times X_k$ is one of the sets X_j, $1 \leq j \leq k$. In the special case where k = 2 and $L \subseteq X_1 \times X_2$ is a function $L : X_1 \rightarrow X_2$, it is conventional to refer to X_1 as the _____ of the function and to refer to X_2 as the codomain of the function.
    a. Domain0
    b. Thing
    c. Undefined
    d. Undefined

6. In mathematics, _____ is the decomposition of an object into a product of other objects, or factors, which when multiplied together give the original.
    a. Thing
    b. Factoring0
    c. Undefined
    d. Undefined

7. _____ element of an element x with respect to a binary operation * with identity element e is an element y such that x * y = y * x = e. In particular,
    a. Inverse0
    b. Thing
    c. Undefined
    d. Undefined

8. In mathematics and logic, a _____ proof is a way of showing the truth or falsehood of a given statement by a straightforward combination of established facts, usually existing lemmas and theorems, without making any further assumptions.
    a. Direct0
    b. Thing
    c. Undefined
    d. Undefined

9. A _____ is the part of a fraction that tells how many equal parts make up a whole, and which is used in the name of the fraction: "halves", "thirds", "fourths" or "quarters", "fifths" and so on.
    a. Denominator0
    b. Concept
    c. Undefined
    d. Undefined

Chapter 6. Rational Expressions and Equations

10. A _____ is a symbolic representation denoting a quantity or expression. It often represents an "unknown" quantity that has the potential to change.
    a. Variable0
    b. Thing
    c. Undefined
    d. Undefined

11. In mathematics, a _____ is an expression that is constructed from one or more variables and constants, using only the operations of addition, subtraction, multiplication, and constant positive whole number exponents. is a _____. Note in particular that division by an expression containing a variable is not in general allowed in polynomials. [1]
    a. Thing
    b. Polynomial0
    c. Undefined
    d. Undefined

12. A _____ is a quantity that denotes the proportional amount or magnitude of one quantity relative to another.
    a. Thing
    b. Ratio0
    c. Undefined
    d. Undefined

13. In mathematics, a _____ may be described informally as a number that can be given by an infinite decimal representation.
    a. Thing
    b. Real number0
    c. Undefined
    d. Undefined

14. In mathematics, a _____ is the end result of a division problem. It can also be expressed as the number of times the divisor divides into the dividend.
    a. Thing
    b. Quotient0
    c. Undefined
    d. Undefined

15. A _____ is a numeral used to indicate a count. The most common use of the word today is to name the part of a fraction that tells the number or count of equal parts.
    a. Numerator0
    b. Thing
    c. Undefined
    d. Undefined

16. In the scientific method, an _____ (Latin: ex-+-periri, "of (or from) trying"), is a set of actions and observations, performed in the context of solving a particular problem or question, in order to support or falsify a hypothesis or research concerning phenomena.
    a. Thing
    b. Experiment0
    c. Undefined
    d. Undefined

17. In mathematics, defined and _____ are used to explain whether or not expressions have meaningful, sensible, and unambiguous values.
    a. Undefined0
    b. Thing
    c. Undefined
    d. Undefined

18. In statistics, _____ means the most frequent value assumed by a random variable, or occurring in a sampling of a random variable.
    a. Mode0
    b. Concept
    c. Undefined
    d. Undefined

19. A _____ is a number that is less than zero.
   a. Thing
   b. Negative number0
   c. Undefined
   d. Undefined

20. _____ is the largest positive integer that divides both numbers without remainder.
   a. Common Factor0
   b. Thing
   c. Undefined
   d. Undefined

21. In mathematics, factorization (British English: factorisation) or factoring is the decomposition of an object (for example, a number, a polynomial, or a matrix) into a product of other objects, or _____, which when multiplied together give the original.
   a. Thing
   b. Factors0
   c. Undefined
   d. Undefined

22. In mathematics, a _____ is the result of multiplying, or an expression that identifies factors to be multiplied.
   a. Thing
   b. Product0
   c. Undefined
   d. Undefined

23. In mathematics, _____ is an elementary arithmetic operation. When one of the numbers is a whole number, _____ is the repeated sum of the other number.
   a. Thing
   b. Multiplication0
   c. Undefined
   d. Undefined

24. In abstract algebra, _____ consists of sets with binary operations that satisfy certain axioms.
   a. Thing
   b. Grouping0
   c. Undefined
   d. Undefined

25. A _____ is a polynomial consisting of three terms; in other words, it is the sum of three monomials.
   a. Trinomial0
   b. Thing
   c. Undefined
   d. Undefined

26. In elementary algebra, a _____ is a polynomial with two terms: the sum of two monomials. It is the simplest kind of polynomial except for a monomial.
   a. Thing
   b. Binomial0
   c. Undefined
   d. Undefined

27. In mathematics, a _____ of an integer n, also called a factor of n, is an integer which evenly divides n without leaving a remainder.
   a. Divisor0
   b. Thing
   c. Undefined
   d. Undefined

28. In common philosophical language, a proposition or _____, is the content of an assertion, that is, it is true-or-false and defined by the meaning of a particular piece of language.
   a. Statement0
   b. Concept
   c. Undefined
   d. Undefined

Chapter 6. Rational Expressions and Equations

29. In geometry, the _____ of an object is a point in some sense in the middle of the object.
    a. Thing
    b. Center0
    c. Undefined
    d. Undefined

30. In Euclidean geometry, an _____ is a closed segment of a differentiable curve in the two-dimensional plane; for example, a circular _____ is a segment of a circle.
    a. Concept
    b. Arc0
    c. Undefined
    d. Undefined

31. _____ or arithmetics is the oldest and most elementary branch of mathematics, used by almost everyone, for tasks ranging from simple daily counting to advanced science and business calculations.
    a. Arithmetic0
    b. Thing
    c. Undefined
    d. Undefined

32. _____ is a natural number that has exactly two distinct natural number divisors, which are 1 and the _____ itself.
    a. Prime number0
    b. Thing
    c. Undefined
    d. Undefined

33. In mathematics, a _____ number (or a _____) is a natural number that has exactly two (distinct) natural number divisors, which are 1 and the _____ number itself.
    a. Prime0
    b. Thing
    c. Undefined
    d. Undefined

34. In mathematics, an inequality is a statement about the relative size or order of two objects. For example 14 > 10, or 14 is _____ 10.
    a. Thing
    b. Greater than0
    c. Undefined
    d. Undefined

35. In mathematics, a _____ is a constant multiplicative factor of a certain object. The object can be such things as a variable, a vector, a function, etc. For example, the _____ of $9x^2$ is 9.
    a. Coefficient0
    b. Thing
    c. Undefined
    d. Undefined

36. In mathematics, a _____ is a particular kind of polynomial, having just one term.
    a. Thing
    b. Monomial0
    c. Undefined
    d. Undefined

37. _____ has many meanings, most of which simply .
    a. Thing
    b. Power0
    c. Undefined
    d. Undefined

38. Equivalence is the condition of being _____ or essentially equal.
    a. Thing
    b. Equivalent0
    c. Undefined
    d. Undefined

Chapter 6. Rational Expressions and Equations

39. In mathematics, _____ expressions is used to reduce the expression into the lowest possible term.
   a. Thing
   b. Simplifying0
   c. Undefined
   d. Undefined

40. In mathematics, the additive inverse, or _____ of a number n is the number that, when added to n, yields zero. The additive inverse of n is denoted −n. For example, 7 is −7, because 7 + (−7) = 0, and the additive inverse of −0.3 is 0.3, because −0.3 + 0.3 = 0.
   a. Opposite0
   b. Thing
   c. Undefined
   d. Undefined

41. In mathematics, the _____ of a number n is the number that, when added to n, yields zero. The _____ of n is denoted −n. For example, 7 is −7, because 7 + (−7) = 0, and the _____ of −0.3 is 0.3, because −0.3 + 0.3 = 0.
   a. Additive inverse0
   b. Thing
   c. Undefined
   d. Undefined

42. In mathematics, the _____ inverse, or opposite, of a number n is the number that, when added to n, yields zero. The _____ inverse of n is denoted −n.
   a. Thing
   b. Additive0
   c. Undefined
   d. Undefined

43. In Euclidean geometry, a _____ is the set of all points in a plane at a fixed distance, called the radius, from a given point, the center.
   a. Circle0
   b. Thing
   c. Undefined
   d. Undefined

44. A _____ of a number is the product of that number with any integer.
   a. Thing
   b. Multiple0
   c. Undefined
   d. Undefined

45. In mathematics, the multiplicative inverse of a number x, denoted 1/x or x^{-1}, is the number which, when multiplied by x, yields 1. The multiplicative inverse of x is also called the _____ of x.
   a. Thing
   b. Reciprocal0
   c. Undefined
   d. Undefined

46. _____, from Latin meaning "to make progress", is defined in two different ways. Pure economic _____ is the increase in wealth that an investor has from making an investment, taking into consideration all costs associated with that investment including the opportunity cost of capital.
   a. Profit0
   b. Thing
   c. Undefined
   d. Undefined

47. _____ is a business term for the amount of money that a company receives from its activities in a given period, mostly from sales of products and/or services to customers
   a. Revenue0
   b. Thing
   c. Undefined
   d. Undefined

Chapter 6. Rational Expressions and Equations

48. An _____ is a straight line or curve A to which another curve B approaches closer and closer as one moves along it. As one moves along B, the space between it and the _____ A becomes smaller and smaller, and can in fact be made as small as one could wish by going far enough along. A curve may or may not touch or cross its _____. In fact, the curve may intersect the _____ an infinite number of times.
   a. Thing
   b. Asymptote0
   c. Undefined
   d. Undefined

49. In mathematics, the _____ of a function is the set of all "output" values produced by that function. Given a function $f : A \to B$, the _____ of f, is defined to be the set $\{x \in B : x = f(a)$ for some $a \in A\}$.
   a. Range0
   b. Thing
   c. Undefined
   d. Undefined

50. The _____ function (weight function) is a mathematical device used when performing a sum, integral, or average in order to give some elements more of a "weight" than others.
   a. Thing
   b. Weighted0
   c. Undefined
   d. Undefined

51. A _____ is often used in statistics.
   a. Weighted mean0
   b. Thing
   c. Undefined
   d. Undefined

52. In mathematics, an _____, mean, or central tendency of a data set refers to a measure of the "middle" or "expected" value of the data set.
   a. Concept
   b. Average0
   c. Undefined
   d. Undefined

53. A _____ is the result of the addition of a set of numbers. The numbers may be natural numbers, complex numbers, matrices, or still more complicated objects. An infinite _____ is a subtle procedure known as a series.
   a. Sum0
   b. Thing
   c. Undefined
   d. Undefined

54. A _____ is a special kind of ratio, indicating a relationship between two measurements with different units, such as miles to gallons or cents to pounds.
   a. Thing
   b. Rate0
   c. Undefined
   d. Undefined

55. In business, particularly accounting, a _____ is the time intervals that the accounts, statement, payments, or other calculations cover.
   a. Thing
   b. Period0
   c. Undefined
   d. Undefined

56. _____ are a measure of time.
   a. Minutes0
   b. Thing
   c. Undefined
   d. Undefined

57. _____ is a mathematical notation for describing a set by stating the properties that its members must satisfy.

Chapter 6. Rational Expressions and Equations

a. Thing
c. Undefined
b. Set-builder notation0
d. Undefined

58. Mathematical _____ is used to represent ideas.
a. Thing
c. Undefined
b. Notation0
d. Undefined

59. _____ is often used to describe the measurement of the steepness, incline, gradient, or grade of a straight line. The _____ is defined as the ratio of the "rise" divided by the "run" between two points on a line, or in other words, the ratio of the altitude change to the horizontal distance between any two points on the line.
a. Thing
c. Undefined
b. Slope0
d. Undefined

60. In algebra, a _____ is a function depending on n that associates a scalar, $det(A)$, to every $n \times n$ square matrix A.
a. Thing
c. Undefined
b. Determinant0
d. Undefined

61. The _____, the average in everyday English, which is also called the arithmetic _____ (and is distinguished from the geometric _____ or harmonic _____). The average is also called the sample _____. The expected value of a random variable, which is also called the population _____.
a. Thing
c. Undefined
b. Mean0
d. Undefined

62. _____ is a mathematical operation, written a^n, involving two numbers, the base a and the exponent n.
a. Thing
c. Undefined
b. Exponentiating0
d. Undefined

63. _____ is a mathematical operation, written a^n, involving two numbers, the base a and the exponent n.
a. Exponentiation0
c. Undefined
b. Thing
d. Undefined

64. In mathematics, and in particular in abstract algebra, the _____ is a property of binary operations that generalises the distributive law from elementary algebra.
a. Thing
c. Undefined
b. Distributive property0
d. Undefined

65. _____ forms part of thinking. Considered the most complex of all intellectual functions, _____ has been defined as higher-order cognitive process that requires the modulation and control of more routine or fundamental skills.
a. Thing
c. Undefined
b. Problem solving0
d. Undefined

66. In geometry, a _____ is defined as a quadrilateral where all four of its angles are right angles.
a. Rectangle0
c. Undefined
b. Thing
d. Undefined

67. In mathematics, _____ is a part of the set theoretic notion of function.

Chapter 6. Rational Expressions and Equations

   a. Thing   b. Image0
   c. Undefined   d. Undefined

68. In elementary algebra, an _____ is a set that contains every real number between two indicated numbers and may contain the two numbers themselves.
   a. Interval0   b. Thing
   c. Undefined   d. Undefined

69. _____ is the notation in which permitted values for a variable are expressed as ranging over a certain interval; "5 < x < 9" is an example of the application of _____.
   a. Interval notation0   b. Thing
   c. Undefined   d. Undefined

70. _____, either of the curved-bracket punctuation marks that together make a set of _____
   a. Thing   b. Parentheses0
   c. Undefined   d. Undefined

71. A _____ is a negotiable instrument instructing a financial institution to pay a specific amount of a specific currency from a specific demand account held in the maker/depositor's name with that institution. Both the maker and payee may be natural persons or legal entities.
   a. Check0   b. Thing
   c. Undefined   d. Undefined

72. _____ variables are variables other than the independent variable that may bear any effect on the behavior of the subject being studied.
   a. Extraneous0   b. Thing
   c. Undefined   d. Undefined

73. In mathematics, a _____ of a complex-valued function f is a member x of the domain of f such that f(x) vanishes at x, that is, x : f (x) = 0.
   a. Root0   b. Thing
   c. Undefined   d. Undefined

74. _____ (or proportionality) are two quantities that vary in such a way that one of the quatities is a constant multiple of the other, or equivalently if they have a constant ratio.
   a. Thing   b. Proportions0
   c. Undefined   d. Undefined

75. _____ is a special mathematical relationship between two quantities. Two quantities are called proportional if they vary in such a way that one of the quantities is a constant multiple of the other, or equivalently if they have a constant ratio.
   a. Proportionality0   b. Thing
   c. Undefined   d. Undefined

76. A _____ is one of the basic shapes of geometry: a polygon with three vertices and three sides which are straight line segments.

Chapter 6. Rational Expressions and Equations

    a. Triangle0   b. Thing
    c. Undefined   d. Undefined

77. _____ is a kind of property which exists as magnitude or multitude. It is among the basic classes of things along with quality, substance, change, and relation.
    a. Amount0   b. Thing
    c. Undefined   d. Undefined

78. _____ is the fee paid on borrowed money.
    a. Thing   b. Interest0
    c. Undefined   d. Undefined

79. An _____ is the fee paid on borrow money.
    a. Interest rate0   b. Concept
    c. Undefined   d. Undefined

80. _____, Greek for "knowledge of nature," is the branch of science concerned with the discovery and characterization of universal laws which govern matter, energy, space, and time.
    a. Thing   b. Physics0
    c. Undefined   d. Undefined

81. In statistics the _____ of an event i is the number n_i of times the event occurred in the experiment or the study. These frequencies are often graphically represented in histograms.
    a. Frequency0   b. Concept
    c. Undefined   d. Undefined

82. A _____ is a deliberate process for transforming one or more inputs into one or more results.
    a. Calculation0   b. Thing
    c. Undefined   d. Undefined

83. _____ is the estimation of a physical quantity such as distance, energy, temperature, or time.
    a. Thing   b. Measurement0
    c. Undefined   d. Undefined

84. In _____ algebra, a *-ring is an associative ring with an antilinear, antiautomorphism * : A ¨ A which is an involution.
    a. Star0   b. Thing
    c. Undefined   d. Undefined

85. The _____ is the change in frequency and wavelength of a wave that is perceived by an observer moving relative to the source of the waves
    a. Doppler Effect0   b. Thing
    c. Undefined   d. Undefined

86. _____ is electromagnetic radiation with a wavelength that is visible to the eye (visible _____) or, in a technical or scientific context, electromagnetic radiation of any wavelength.

Chapter 6. Rational Expressions and Equations

a. Thing
b. Light0
c. Undefined
d. Undefined

87. The plus and _____ signs are mathematical symbols used to represent the notions of positive and negative as well as the operations of addition and subtraction.
a. Thing
b. Minus0
c. Undefined
d. Undefined

88. _____, in law and economics, is a form of risk management primarily used to hedge against the risk of a contingent loss.
a. Insurance0
b. Thing
c. Undefined
d. Undefined

89. A _____ is a plan of action to guide decisions and actions.
a. Policy0
b. Thing
c. Undefined
d. Undefined

90. _____ is the transport of people on a trip/journey or the process or time involved in a person or object moving from one location to another.
a. Thing
b. Travel0
c. Undefined
d. Undefined

91. _____ of an object is its speed in a particular direction.
a. Velocity0
b. Thing
c. Undefined
d. Undefined

92. A _____ is a unit of length, usually used to measure distance, in a number of different systems, including Imperial units, United States customary units and Norwegian/Swedish mil. Its size can vary from system to system, but in each is between 1 and 10 kilometers. In contemporary English contexts _____ refers to either:
a. Mile0
b. Thing
c. Undefined
d. Undefined

93. _____ or investing is a term with several closely-related meanings in business management, finance and economics, related to saving or deferring consumption.
a. Thing
b. Investment0
c. Undefined
d. Undefined

94. _____ is defined as the rate of change or derivative with respect to time of velocity.
a. Thing
b. Acceleration0
c. Undefined
d. Undefined

95. The _____ of measurement are a globally standardized and modernized form of the metric system.
a. Thing
b. Units0
c. Undefined
d. Undefined

96. The _____ rule, also known as a slipstick, is a mechanical analog computer, consisting of at least two finely divided scales, most often a fixed outer pair and a movable inner one, with a sliding window called the cursor.
   a. Slide0
   b. Thing
   c. Undefined
   d. Undefined

97. In mathematics, the concept of a _____ tries to capture the intuitive idea of a geometrical one-dimensional and continuous object. A simple example is the circle.
   a. Curve0
   b. Thing
   c. Undefined
   d. Undefined

98. In mathematics, a _____ is an algebraic structure in which addition and multiplication are defined and have properties listed below.
   a. Ring0
   b. Thing
   c. Undefined
   d. Undefined

99. In physics, an _____ is the path that an object makes around another object while under the influence of a source of centripetal force, such as gravity.
   a. Thing
   b. Orbit0
   c. Undefined
   d. Undefined

100. A _____, as defined by the International Astronomical Union, is a celestial body orbiting a star or stellar remnant that is massive enough to be rounded by its own gravity, not massive enough to cause thermonuclear fusion in its core, and has cleared its neighboring region of planetesimals.
   a. Planet0
   b. Thing
   c. Undefined
   d. Undefined

101. In mathematics, a _____ is a two-dimensional manifold or surface that is perfectly flat.
   a. Thing
   b. Plane0
   c. Undefined
   d. Undefined

102. The metre (or _____, see spelling differences) is a measure of length. It is the basic unit of length in the metric system and in the International System of Units (SI), used around the world for general and scientific purposes.
   a. Meter0
   b. Concept
   c. Undefined
   d. Undefined

103. In mathematics, an _____ is a statement about the relative size or order of two objects.
   a. Inequality0
   b. Thing
   c. Undefined
   d. Undefined

104. In plane geometry, a _____ is a polygon with four equal sides, four right angles, and parallel opposite sides. In algebra, the _____ of a number is that number multiplied by itself.
   a. Square0
   b. Thing
   c. Undefined
   d. Undefined

105. A _____ is 360° or 2∂ radians.

Chapter 6. Rational Expressions and Equations

    a. Thing   b. Turn0
    c. Undefined   d. Undefined

106. In mathematics and more specifically set theory, the _____ set is the unique set which contains no elements.
    a. Empty0   b. Thing
    c. Undefined   d. Undefined

107. In geometry, an _____ of a triangle is a straight line through a vertex and perpendicular to (i.e. forming a right angle with) the opposite side or an extension of the opposite side.
    a. Altitude0   b. Concept
    c. Undefined   d. Undefined

108. _____ is a unit of speed, expressing the number of international miles covered per hour.
    a. Miles per hour0   b. Thing
    c. Undefined   d. Undefined

109. In botany, _____ are above-ground plant organs specialized for photosynthesis. Their characteristics are typically analyzed by using Fiobonacci's sequences.
    a. Thing   b. Leaves0
    c. Undefined   d. Undefined

110. The _____ are the only integral domain whose positive elements are well-ordered, and in which order is preserved by addition. Like the natural numbers, the _____ form a countably infinite set. The set of all _____ is usually denoted in mathematics by a boldface Z .
    a. Integers0   b. Thing
    c. Undefined   d. Undefined

111. _____ means in succession or back-to-back
    a. Thing   b. Consecutive0
    c. Undefined   d. Undefined

112. A _____ given two distinct points A and B on the _____, is the set of points C on the line containing points A and B such that A is not strictly between C and B.
    a. Thing   b. Ray0
    c. Undefined   d. Undefined

113. A _____ is a unit of length in the metric system, equal to one thousand metres, the current SI base unit of length
    a. Thing   b. Kilometer0
    c. Undefined   d. Undefined

114. In set theory and other branches of mathematics, the _____ of a collection of sets is the set that contains everything that belongs to any of the sets, but nothing else.
    a. Union0   b. Thing
    c. Undefined   d. Undefined

115. A _____ is a type of bridge that has been created since ancient times as early as 100 AD.

Chapter 6. Rational Expressions and Equations

   a. Thing
   c. Undefined
   b. Suspension bridge0
   d. Undefined

116. A _____ is a landform that extends above the surrounding terrain in a limited area. A _____ is generally steeper than a hill, but there is no universally accepted standard definition for the height of a _____ or a hill although a _____ usually has an identifiable summit.
   a. Thing
   c. Undefined
   b. Mountain0
   d. Undefined

117. _____ is a set, with some particular properties and usually some additional structure, such as the operations of addition or multiplication, for instance.
   a. Space0
   c. Undefined
   b. Thing
   d. Undefined

118. _____ is the largest city in the state of Texas and the fourth-largest in the United States. As of the 2005 U.S. Census estimate, it had a population of more than 2 million.
   a. Houston0
   c. Undefined
   b. Thing
   d. Undefined

119. A _____ is a vehicle, missile or aircraft which obtains thrust by the reaction to the ejection of fast moving fluid from within a _____ engine.
   a. Rocket0
   c. Undefined
   b. Thing
   d. Undefined

120. _____ is a state located in the southern and southwestern regions of the United States of America.
   a. Thing
   c. Undefined
   b. Texas0
   d. Undefined

121. _____ is a notation for writing numbers that is often used by scientists and mathematicians to make it easier to write large and small numbers.
   a. Thing
   c. Undefined
   b. Scientific notation0
   d. Undefined

122. _____ is a form of periodic payment from an employer to an employee, which is specified in an employment contract.
   a. Gross pay0
   c. Undefined
   b. Thing
   d. Undefined

123. The payment of _____ as remuneration for services rendered or products sold is a common way to reward sales people.
   a. Thing
   c. Undefined
   b. Commission0
   d. Undefined

124. A _____ is a form of periodic payment from an employer to an employee, which is specified in an employment contract.

Chapter 6. Rational Expressions and Equations

    a. Thing
    c. Undefined
    b. Salary0
    d. Undefined

125. The _____ of a solid object is the three-dimensional concept of how much space it occupies, often quantified numerically.
    a. Thing
    c. Undefined
    b. Volume0
    d. Undefined

126. _____ is a relationship among three or more variables in which each pair of variables varies directly or inversely.
    a. Thing
    c. Undefined
    b. Joint variation0
    d. Undefined

127. _____ is the relationship between two variables, like a ratio in which the two quantities being compared are different units.
    a. Thing
    c. Undefined
    b. Direct variation0
    d. Undefined

128. In mathematics, two quantities are called _____ if they vary in such a way that one of the quantities is a constant multiple of the other, or equivalently if they have a constant ratio.
    a. Thing
    c. Undefined
    b. Proportional0
    d. Undefined

129. In classical geometry, a _____ of a circle or sphere is any line segment from its center to its boundary. By extension, the _____ of a circle or sphere is the length of any such segment. The _____ is half the diameter. In science and engineering the term _____ of curvature is commonly used as a synonym for _____.
    a. Radius0
    c. Undefined
    b. Thing
    d. Undefined

130. The _____ is the distance around a closed curve. _____ is a kind of perimeter.
    a. Circumference0
    c. Undefined
    b. Thing
    d. Undefined

131. _____ is the property of a physical object that quantifies the amount of matter and energy it is equivalent to.
    a. Mass0
    c. Undefined
    b. Thing
    d. Undefined

132. In mathematics and the mathematical sciences, a _____ is a fixed, but possibly unspecified, value. This is in contrast to a variable, which is not fixed.
    a. Constant0
    c. Undefined
    b. Thing
    d. Undefined

133. The _____ or kilogramme is the SI base unit of mass. It is defined as being equal to the mass of the international prototype of the _____.
    a. Kilogram0
    c. Undefined
    b. Thing
    d. Undefined

Chapter 6. Rational Expressions and Equations

134. _____ is a physical property of a system that underlies the common notions of hot and cold; something that is hotter has the greater _____.
   a. Temperature0
   b. Thing
   c. Undefined
   d. Undefined

135. In combinatorial mathematics, a _____ is an un-ordered collection of unique elements.
   a. Combination0
   b. Concept
   c. Undefined
   d. Undefined

136. In physics, _____ is an influence that may cause an object to accelerate. It may be experienced as a lift, a push, or a pull. The actual acceleration of the body is determined by the vector sum of all forces acting on it, known as net _____ or resultant _____.
   a. Force0
   b. Thing
   c. Undefined
   d. Undefined

137. A _____ is a method of using property as security for the payment of a debt.
   a. Mortgage0
   b. Thing
   c. Undefined
   d. Undefined

138. _____ is electric power as defined as the amount of work done by an electric current, or the rate at which electrical energy is transferred.
   a. Wattage0
   b. Thing
   c. Undefined
   d. Undefined

139. In sociology and biology a _____ is the collection of people or organisms of a particular species living in a given geographic area or space, usually measured by a census.
   a. Population0
   b. Thing
   c. Undefined
   d. Undefined

140. In mathematics, a _____ of a number x is a number r such that $r^2 = x$, or in words, a number r whose square (the result of multiplying the number by itself) is x.
   a. Thing
   b. Square root0
   c. Undefined
   d. Undefined

141. _____ is the process of recording pictures by means of capturing light on a light-sensitive medium, such as a film or sensor.
   a. Thing
   b. Photography0
   c. Undefined
   d. Undefined

142. Sir Isaac _____, was an English physicist, mathematician, astronomer, natural philosopher, and alchemist, regarded by many as the greatest figure in the history of science
   a. Newton0
   b. Person
   c. Undefined
   d. Undefined

143. In mathematics, a matrix can be thought of as each row or _____ being a vector. Hence, a space formed by row vectors or _____ vectors are said to be a row space or a _____ space.

Chapter 6. Rational Expressions and Equations

a. Column0
b. Concept
c. Undefined
d. Undefined

144. A _____ is a three-dimensional solid object bounded by six square faces, facets, or sides, with three meeting at each vertex.
 a. Cube0
 b. Thing
 c. Undefined
 d. Undefined

145. Acid _____ ratio measures the ability of a company to use its near cash or quick assets to immediately extinguish its current liabilities.
 a. Test0
 b. Thing
 c. Undefined
 d. Undefined

146. A _____ is a one-dimensional picture in which the integers are shown as specially-marked points evenly spaced on a line.
 a. Thing
 b. Number line0
 c. Undefined
 d. Undefined

147. In mathematics, there are several meanings of _____ depending on the subject.
 a. Thing
 b. Degree0
 c. Undefined
 d. Undefined

148. A _____ or CD is a time deposit, a financial product commonly offered to consumers by banks, thrift institutions, and credit unions.
 a. Certificate of deposit0
 b. Thing
 c. Undefined
 d. Undefined

149. _____ is the symbold used to indicate the nth root of a number
 a. Thing
 b. Radical0
 c. Undefined
 d. Undefined

150. In mathematics, _____ are used to indicate the square root of a number.
 a. Thing
 b. Radicals0
 c. Undefined
 d. Undefined

Chapter 7. Roots, Radicals, and Complex Numbers

1. A _____ is a three-dimensional solid object bounded by six square faces, facets, or sides, with three meeting at each vertex.
   a. Cube0
   b. Thing
   c. Undefined
   d. Undefined

2. A _____ of a number is a number a such that $a^3 = x$.
   a. Cube root0
   b. Thing
   c. Undefined
   d. Undefined

3. In plane geometry, a _____ is a polygon with four equal sides, four right angles, and parallel opposite sides. In algebra, the _____ of a number is that number multiplied by itself.
   a. Square0
   b. Thing
   c. Undefined
   d. Undefined

4. In mathematics, a _____ of a number x is a number r such that $r^2 = x$, or in words, a number r whose square (the result of multiplying the number by itself) is x.
   a. Square root0
   b. Thing
   c. Undefined
   d. Undefined

5. In mathematics, a _____ of a complex-valued function f is a member x of the domain of f such that f(x) vanishes at x, that is, x : f (x) = 0.
   a. Thing
   b. Root0
   c. Undefined
   d. Undefined

6. The mathematical concept of a _____ expresses the intuitive idea of deterministic dependence between two quantities, one of which is viewed as primary and the other as secondary. A _____ then is a way to associate a unique output for each input of a specified type, for example, a real number or an element of a given set.
   a. Function0
   b. Thing
   c. Undefined
   d. Undefined

7. _____ is the symbol used to indicate the nth root of a number
   a. Thing
   b. Radical0
   c. Undefined
   d. Undefined

8. In mathematics, _____ growth occurs when the growth rate of a function is always proportional to the function's current size.
   a. Thing
   b. Exponential0
   c. Undefined
   d. Undefined

9. An _____ is a combination of numbers, operators, grouping symbols and/or free variables and bound variables arranged in a meaningful way which can be evaluated..
   a. Thing
   b. Expression0
   c. Undefined
   d. Undefined

10. In mathematics, _____ expressions is used to reduce the expression into the lowest possible term.

Chapter 7. Roots, Radicals, and Complex Numbers

a. Simplifying0
b. Thing
c. Undefined
d. Undefined

11. In mathematics, _____ are used to indicate the square root of a number.
    a. Radicals0
    b. Thing
    c. Undefined
    d. Undefined

12. _____, or Rationalisation in mathematics is the process of removing a square root or imaginary number from the denominator of a fraction.
    a. Rationalizing0
    b. Thing
    c. Undefined
    d. Undefined

13. A _____ is the part of a fraction that tells how many equal parts make up a whole, and which is used in the name of the fraction: "halves", "thirds", "fourths" or "quarters", "fifths" and so on.
    a. Concept
    b. Denominator0
    c. Undefined
    d. Undefined

14. In mathematics, an _____ number is a complex number whose square is a negative real number. They were defined in 1572 by Rafael Bombelli.
    a. Thing
    b. Imaginary0
    c. Undefined
    d. Undefined

15. In mathematics, a _____ is a number in the form of a + bi where a and b are real numbers, and i is the imaginary unit, with the property i 2 = −1. The real number a is called the real part of the _____, and the real number b is the imaginary part.
    a. Thing
    b. Complex number0
    c. Undefined
    d. Undefined

16. In mathematics, the _____ (or modulus) of a real number is its numerical value without regard to its sign.
    a. Absolute value0
    b. Thing
    c. Undefined
    d. Undefined

17. The _____ is the number or expression underneath the radical sign.
    a. Thing
    b. Radicand0
    c. Undefined
    d. Undefined

18. The word _____ is used in a variety of ways in mathematics.
    a. Thing
    b. Index0
    c. Undefined
    d. Undefined

19. In mathematics, a _____ number is a number which can be expressed as a ratio of two integers. Non-integer _____ numbers (commonly called fractions) are usually written as the vulgar fraction a / b, where b is not zero.
    a. Rational0
    b. Thing
    c. Undefined
    d. Undefined

Chapter 7. Roots, Radicals, and Complex Numbers

20. A _____ decimal is a number whose decimal representation eventually becomes periodic (i.e. the same number sequence _____ indefinitely).
    a. Thing
    b. Repeating0
    c. Undefined
    d. Undefined

21. A _____ decimal is a decimal fraction which ends after a definite number of digits.
    a. Thing
    b. Terminating0
    c. Undefined
    d. Undefined

22. A _____ decimal is a decimal for which there is no digit to the right of the decimal point, as all digits farther from the right are zero.
    a. Thing
    b. Nonterminating0
    c. Undefined
    d. Undefined

23. A _____ is a number that is less than zero.
    a. Thing
    b. Negative number0
    c. Undefined
    d. Undefined

24. In mathematics, a _____ may be described informally as a number that can be given by an infinite decimal representation.
    a. Real number0
    b. Thing
    c. Undefined
    d. Undefined

25. In mathematics, the additive inverse, or _____ of a number n is the number that, when added to n, yields zero. The additive inverse of n is denoted −n. For example, 7 is −7, because 7 + (−7) = 0, and the additive inverse of −0.3 is 0.3, because −0.3 + 0.3 = 0.
    a. Thing
    b. Opposite0
    c. Undefined
    d. Undefined

26. In mathematics, the _____ of a number n is the number that, when added to n, yields zero. The _____ of n is denoted −n. For example, 7 is −7, because 7 + (−7) = 0, and the _____ of −0.3 is 0.3, because −0.3 + 0.3 = 0.
    a. Thing
    b. Additive inverse0
    c. Undefined
    d. Undefined

27. In mathematics, a _____ of a k-place relation $L \subseteq X_1 \times ... \times X_k$ is one of the sets X_j, $1 \leq j \leq k$. In the special case where k = 2 and $L \subseteq X_1 \times X_2$ is a function $L : X_1 \to X_2$, it is conventional to refer to X_1 as the _____ of the function and to refer to X_2 as the codomain of the function.
    a. Thing
    b. Domain0
    c. Undefined
    d. Undefined

28. The _____ integers are all the integers from zero on upwards.
    a. Nonnegative0
    b. Thing
    c. Undefined
    d. Undefined

29. An _____ of a number a is a number b such that $b^n = a$.

a. Nth root0
b. Thing
c. Undefined
d. Undefined

30. A _____ is a symbolic representation denoting a quantity or expression. It often represents an "unknown" quantity that has the potential to change.
   a. Variable0
   b. Thing
   c. Undefined
   d. Undefined

31. A _____ is a polynomial consisting of three terms; in other words, it is the sum of three monomials.
   a. Thing
   b. Trinomial0
   c. Undefined
   d. Undefined

32. The term _____ can refer to an integer which is the square of some other integer, or an algebraic expression that can be factored as the square of some other expression.
   a. Perfect square0
   b. Thing
   c. Undefined
   d. Undefined

33. In mathematics, an _____ number is any real number that is not a rational number- that is, it is a number which cannot be expressed as a fraction m/n, where m and n are integers.
   a. Thing
   b. Irrational0
   c. Undefined
   d. Undefined

34. In mathematics, an _____ is any real number that is not a rational number ¡ª that is, it is a number which cannot be expressed as m/n, where m and n are integers.
   a. Irrational number0
   b. Thing
   c. Undefined
   d. Undefined

35. In mathematics, _____ are any real number that is not a rational number ¡ª that is, it is a number which cannot be expressed as m/n, where m and n are integers.
   a. Thing
   b. Irrational numbers0
   c. Undefined
   d. Undefined

36. _____ is the property of a physical object that quantifies the amount of matter and energy it is equivalent to.
   a. Thing
   b. Mass0
   c. Undefined
   d. Undefined

37. A _____ is a negotiable instrument instructing a financial institution to pay a specific amount of a specific currency from a specific demand account held in the maker/depositor's name with that institution. Both the maker and payee may be natural persons or legal entities.
   a. Check0
   b. Thing
   c. Undefined
   d. Undefined

38. In mathematics, _____ is an elementary arithmetic operation. When one of the numbers is a whole number, _____ is the repeated sum of the other number.

Chapter 7. Roots, Radicals, and Complex Numbers

    a. Multiplication0   b. Thing
    c. Undefined   d. Undefined

39. _____ is a mathematical operation, written a^n, involving two numbers, the base a and the exponent n.
    a. Exponentiating0   b. Thing
    c. Undefined   d. Undefined

40. _____ is a mathematical operation, written a^n, involving two numbers, the base a and the exponent n.
    a. Thing   b. Exponentiation0
    c. Undefined   d. Undefined

41. A _____ is a numeral used to indicate a count. The most common use of the word today is to name the part of a fraction that tells the number or count of equal parts.
    a. Thing   b. Numerator0
    c. Undefined   d. Undefined

42. _____ has many meanings, most of which simply .
    a. Power0   b. Thing
    c. Undefined   d. Undefined

43. In mathematics, a _____ is the result of multiplying, or an expression that identifies factors to be multiplied.
    a. Thing   b. Product0
    c. Undefined   d. Undefined

44. In mathematics, a _____ is the end result of a division problem. It can also be expressed as the number of times the divisor divides into the dividend.
    a. Quotient0   b. Thing
    c. Undefined   d. Undefined

45. A _____ signifies a point or points of probability on a subject e.g., the _____ of creativity, which allows for the formation of rule or norm or law by interpretation of the phenomena events that can be created.
    a. Thing   b. Principle0
    c. Undefined   d. Undefined

46. The _____, the average in everyday English, which is also called the arithmetic _____ (and is distinguished from the geometric _____ or harmonic _____). The average is also called the sample _____. The expected value of a random variable, which is also called the population _____.
    a. Thing   b. Mean0
    c. Undefined   d. Undefined

47. The _____ governs the differentiation of products of differentiable functions.
    a. Thing   b. Product rule0
    c. Undefined   d. Undefined

48. In mathematics, and in particular in abstract algebra, the _____ is a property of binary operations that generalises the distributive law from elementary algebra.

Chapter 7. Roots, Radicals, and Complex Numbers   101

a. Distributive property0
b. Thing
c. Undefined
d. Undefined

49. In mathematics, _____ is the decomposition of an object into a product of other objects, or factors, which when multiplied together give the original.
    a. Thing
    b. Factoring0
    c. Undefined
    d. Undefined

50. _____ is a physical property of a system that underlies the common notions of hot and cold; something that is hotter has the greater _____.
    a. Thing
    b. Temperature0
    c. Undefined
    d. Undefined

51. A _____ fraction is a fraction in which the absolute value of the numerator is less than the denominator--hence, the absolute value of the fraction is less than 1.
    a. Proper0
    b. Thing
    c. Undefined
    d. Undefined

52. _____ is a term applied when talking about the movement of air from one place to the next.
    a. Wind speed0
    b. Thing
    c. Undefined
    d. Undefined

53. _____ of an object is its speed in a particular direction.
    a. Thing
    b. Velocity0
    c. Undefined
    d. Undefined

54. In mathematics, there are several meanings of _____ depending on the subject.
    a. Degree0
    b. Thing
    c. Undefined
    d. Undefined

55. A _____ is a unit of length, usually used to measure distance, in a number of different systems, including Imperial units, United States customary units and Norwegian/Swedish mil. Its size can vary from system to system, but in each is between 1 and 10 kilometers. In contemporary English contexts _____ refers to either:
    a. Thing
    b. Mile0
    c. Undefined
    d. Undefined

56. _____ is a unit of speed, expressing the number of international miles covered per hour.
    a. Thing
    b. Miles per hour0
    c. Undefined
    d. Undefined

57. _____ is a radiometric dating method that uses the naturally occurring isotope carbon-14 to determine the age of carbonaceous materials up to about 60,000 years.
    a. Thing
    b. Radiocarbon dating0
    c. Undefined
    d. Undefined

Chapter 7. Roots, Radicals, and Complex Numbers

58. _____ is a kind of property which exists as magnitude or multitude. It is among the basic classes of things along with quality, substance, change, and relation.
   a. Amount0
   b. Thing
   c. Undefined
   d. Undefined

59. In common philosophical language, a proposition or _____, is the content of an assertion, that is, it is true-or-false and defined by the meaning of a particular piece of language.
   a. Concept
   b. Statement0
   c. Undefined
   d. Undefined

60. In mathematics, a _____ is a two-dimensional manifold or surface that is perfectly flat.
   a. Plane0
   b. Thing
   c. Undefined
   d. Undefined

61. The _____ is a method of finding the derivative of a function that is the quotient of two other functions for which derivatives exist.
   a. Quotient rule0
   b. Thing
   c. Undefined
   d. Undefined

62. A _____ of a number is the product of that number with any integer.
   a. Thing
   b. Multiple0
   c. Undefined
   d. Undefined

63. _____ are of a number n in its third power-the result of multiplying it by itself three times.
   a. Thing
   b. Cubes0
   c. Undefined
   d. Undefined

64. A _____ is a number which is the cube of an integer.
   a. Perfect cube0
   b. Thing
   c. Undefined
   d. Undefined

65. In mathematics, a _____ of an integer n, also called a factor of n, is an integer which evenly divides n without leaving a remainder.
   a. Thing
   b. Divisor0
   c. Undefined
   d. Undefined

66. In mathematics, a _____ is a constant multiplicative factor of a certain object. The object can be such things as a variable, a vector, a function, etc. For example, the _____ of $9x^2$ is 9.
   a. Thing
   b. Coefficient0
   c. Undefined
   d. Undefined

67. In mathematics, factorization (British English: factorisation) or factoring is the decomposition of an object (for example, a number, a polynomial, or a matrix) into a product of other objects, or _____, which when multiplied together give the original.

Chapter 7. Roots, Radicals, and Complex Numbers

    a. Factors0   b. Thing
    c. Undefined   d. Undefined

68. A _____ is the result of the addition of a set of numbers. The numbers may be natural numbers, complex numbers, matrices, or still more complicated objects. An infinite _____ is a subtle procedure known as a series.
    a. Thing   b. Sum0
    c. Undefined   d. Undefined

69. In mathematics, an inequality is a statement about the relative size or order of two objects. For example 14 > 10, or 14 is _____ 10.
    a. Greater than0   b. Thing
    c. Undefined   d. Undefined

70. A _____ is the part of the dividend that is left over when the dividend is not evenly divisible by the divisor.
    a. Remainder0   b. Thing
    c. Undefined   d. Undefined

71. In mathematics, a _____ can mean either an element of the set {1, 2, 3, ...} (i.e the positive integers or the counting numbers) or an element of the set {0, 1, 2, 3, ...} (i.e. the non-negative integers).
    a. Natural number0   b. Thing
    c. Undefined   d. Undefined

72. In elementary algebra, a _____ is a polynomial with two terms: the sum of two monomials. It is the simplest kind of polynomial except for a monomial.
    a. Binomial0   b. Thing
    c. Undefined   d. Undefined

73. _____ also sometimes known as the double distributive property or more colloquially as foiling, is commonly taught to US high school students learning algebra as a mnemonic for remembering how to multiply two binomials polynomials with two terms.
    a. FOIL method0   b. Thing
    c. Undefined   d. Undefined

74. The _____ is commonly taught to US high school students learning algebra as a mnemonic for remembering how to multiply two binomials.
    a. Thing   b. FOIL rule0
    c. Undefined   d. Undefined

75. A _____ is a special kind of ratio, indicating a relationship between two measurements with different units, such as miles to gallons or cents to pounds.
    a. Thing   b. Rate0
    c. Undefined   d. Undefined

Chapter 7. Roots, Radicals, and Complex Numbers

76. In geometry, a _____ (Greek words diairo = divide and metro = measure) of a circle is any straight line segment that passes through the centre and whose endpoints are on the circular boundary, or, in more modern usage, the length of such a line segment. When using the word in the more modern sense, one speaks of the _____ rather than a _____, because all diameters of a circle have the same length. This length is twice the radius. The _____ of a circle is also the longest chord that the circle has.
   a. Diameter0
   b. Thing
   c. Undefined
   d. Undefined

77. In probability theory and statistics, a _____ is a number dividing the higher half of a sample, a population, or a probability distribution from the lower half.
   a. Median0
   b. Concept
   c. Undefined
   d. Undefined

78. _____ is the eighteenth letter of the Greek alphabet.
   a. Sigma0
   b. Thing
   c. Undefined
   d. Undefined

79. _____ of a probability distribution, random variable, or population or multiset of values is a measure of the spread of its values.
   a. Standard deviation0
   b. Thing
   c. Undefined
   d. Undefined

80. _____ is a mathematical science pertaining to the collection, analysis, interpretation or explanation, and presentation of data. It is applicable to a wide variety of academic disciplines, from the physical and social sciences to the humanities.
   a. Statistics0
   b. Thing
   c. Undefined
   d. Undefined

81. _____ is a synonym for information.
   a. Thing
   b. Data0
   c. Undefined
   d. Undefined

82. A _____ is a function that assigns a number to subsets of a given set.
   a. Thing
   b. Measure0
   c. Undefined
   d. Undefined

83. In sociology and biology a _____ is the collection of people or organisms of a particular species living in a given geographic area or space, usually measured by a census.
   a. Thing
   b. Population0
   c. Undefined
   d. Undefined

84. _____ is a measure of difference for interval and ratio variables between the observed value and the mean.
   a. Deviation0
   b. Thing
   c. Undefined
   d. Undefined

85. _____ is the chance that something is likely to happen or be the case.

Chapter 7. Roots, Radicals, and Complex Numbers

a. Thing
b. Probability0
c. Undefined
d. Undefined

86. _____ is a way of expressing a number as a fraction of 100 per cent meaning "per hundred".
   a. Percent0
   b. Thing
   c. Undefined
   d. Undefined

87. _____ is a subset of a population.
   a. Thing
   b. Sample0
   c. Undefined
   d. Undefined

88. Mathematical _____ is used to represent ideas.
   a. Notation0
   b. Thing
   c. Undefined
   d. Undefined

89. In geometry, the _____ of an object is a point in some sense in the middle of the object.
   a. Thing
   b. Center0
   c. Undefined
   d. Undefined

90. The _____ of measurement are a globally standardized and modernized form of the metric system.
   a. Units0
   b. Thing
   c. Undefined
   d. Undefined

91. In algebra, a _____ is a binomial formed by taking the opposite of the second term of a binomial.
   a. Conjugate0
   b. Thing
   c. Undefined
   d. Undefined

92. In mathematics, the _____ of continuity is a precise way to measure the smoothness of a function.
   a. Thing
   b. Modulus0
   c. Undefined
   d. Undefined

93. Acid _____ ratio measures the ability of a company to use its near cash or quick assets to immediately extinguish its current liabilities.
   a. Test0
   b. Thing
   c. Undefined
   d. Undefined

94. In mathematics and the mathematical sciences, a _____ is a fixed, but possibly unspecified, value. This is in contrast to a variable, which is not fixed.
   a. Constant0
   b. Thing
   c. Undefined
   d. Undefined

95. The _____ of a solid object is the three-dimensional concept of how much space it occupies, often quantified numerically.
   a. Volume0
   b. Thing
   c. Undefined
   d. Undefined

96. In classical geometry, a _____ of a circle or sphere is any line segment from its center to its boundary. By extension, the _____ of a circle or sphere is the length of any such segment. The _____ is half the diameter. In science and engineering the term _____ of curvature is commonly used as a synonym for _____.
  a. Radius0
  b. Thing
  c. Undefined
  d. Undefined

97. _____ is the transport of people on a trip/journey or the process or time involved in a person or object moving from one location to another.
  a. Thing
  b. Travel0
  c. Undefined
  d. Undefined

98. _____ variables are variables other than the independent variable that may bear any effect on the behavior of the subject being studied.
  a. Extraneous0
  b. Thing
  c. Undefined
  d. Undefined

99. A _____ is an object that is attached to a pivot point so that it can swing freely.
  a. Pendulum0
  b. Thing
  c. Undefined
  d. Undefined

100. In business, particularly accounting, a _____ is the time intervals that the accounts, statement, payments, or other calculations cover.
  a. Thing
  b. Period0
  c. Undefined
  d. Undefined

101. A _____ is one of the basic shapes of geometry: a polygon with three vertices and three sides which are straight line segments.
  a. Thing
  b. Triangle0
  c. Undefined
  d. Undefined

102. _____ has one 90° internal angle a right angle.
  a. Right triangle0
  b. Thing
  c. Undefined
  d. Undefined

103. In mathematics, a _____ is a statement that can be proved on the basis of explicitly stated or previously agreed assumptions.
  a. Theorem0
  b. Thing
  c. Undefined
  d. Undefined

104. The metre (or _____, see spelling differences) is a measure of length. It is the basic unit of length in the metric system and in the International System of Units (SI), used around the world for general and scientific purposes.
  a. Meter0
  b. Concept
  c. Undefined
  d. Undefined

105. In Euclidean geometry, a _____ is the set of all points in a plane at a fixed distance, called the radius, from a given point, the center.

a. Thing
b. Circle0
c. Undefined
d. Undefined

106. _____ is defined as the rate of change or derivative with respect to time of velocity.
   a. Acceleration0
   b. Thing
   c. Undefined
   d. Undefined

107. A _____ can refer to a line joining two nonadjacent vertices of a polygon or polyhedron, or in some contexts any upward or downward sloping line. .
   a. Thing
   b. Diagonal0
   c. Undefined
   d. Undefined

108. _____ is the flow of blood in the cardiovascular system.
   a. Thing
   b. Blood flow0
   c. Undefined
   d. Undefined

109. A _____, as defined by the International Astronomical Union , is a celestial body orbiting a star or stellar remnant that is massive enough to be rounded by its own gravity, not massive enough to cause thermonuclear fusion in its core, and has cleared its neighboring region of planetesimals.
   a. Thing
   b. Planet0
   c. Undefined
   d. Undefined

110. A _____ is a unit of length in the metric system, equal to one thousand metres, the current SI base unit of length
   a. Thing
   b. Kilometer0
   c. Undefined
   d. Undefined

111. In physics, _____ is an influence that may cause an object to accelerate. It may be experienced as a lift, a push, or a pull. The actual acceleration of the body is determined by the vector sum of all forces acting on it, known as net _____ or resultant _____.
   a. Force0
   b. Thing
   c. Undefined
   d. Undefined

112. For a given gravitational field and a given position, the _____ is the minimum speed an object without propulsion needs to have to move away indefinitely from the source of the field, as opposed to falling back or staying in an orbit within a bounded distance from the source.
   a. Thing
   b. Escape velocity0
   c. Undefined
   d. Undefined

113. A _____, or Ocean Surface Waves are surface waves that occur in the upper layer of the ocean.
   a. Water wave0
   b. Thing
   c. Undefined
   d. Undefined

114. _____ is the disturbance that propagates through space or spacetime, often transferring energy.
   a. Thing
   b. Wave motion0
   c. Undefined
   d. Undefined

Chapter 7. Roots, Radicals, and Complex Numbers

115. Sound is a disturbance of mechanical energy that propagates through matter as a wave or _____.
   a. Sound wave0
   b. Thing
   c. Undefined
   d. Undefined

116. A quadratic equation with real solutions, called roots, which may be real or complex, is given by the _____: $x = \frac{-b \pm \sqrt{b^2 - 4ac}}{2a}$.
   a. Thing
   b. Quadratic formula0
   c. Undefined
   d. Undefined

117. Equivalence is the condition of being _____ or essentially equal.
   a. Equivalent0
   b. Thing
   c. Undefined
   d. Undefined

118. _____ is, or relates to, the _____ temperature scale .
   a. Thing
   b. Celsius0
   c. Undefined
   d. Undefined

119. In mathematics, the _____ of a function is the set of all "output" values produced by that function. Given a function $f : A \to B$, the _____ of f, is defined to be the set $\{x \in B : x = f(a) \text{ for some } a \in A\}$.
   a. Thing
   b. Range0
   c. Undefined
   d. Undefined

120. In statistics, a _____ for a population parameter is an interval with an associated probability p that is generated from a random sample of an underlying population such that if the sampling was repeated numerous times and the _____ recalculated from each sample according to the same method, a proportion p of the confidence intervals would contain the population parameter in question.
   a. Thing
   b. Confidence interval0
   c. Undefined
   d. Undefined

121. In elementary algebra, an _____ is a set that contains every real number between two indicated numbers and may contain the two numbers themselves.
   a. Thing
   b. Interval0
   c. Undefined
   d. Undefined

122. _____ is the difference of electrical potential between two points of an electrical or electronic circuit, expressed in volts
   a. Voltage0
   b. Thing
   c. Undefined
   d. Undefined

123. In mathematical analysis, _____ are objects which generalize functions and probability distributions.
   a. Thing
   b. Distribution0
   c. Undefined
   d. Undefined

124. In geometry, a _____ is a special kind of point, usually a corner of a polygon, polyhedron, or higher dimensional polytope. In the geometry of curves a _____ is a point of where the first derivative of curvature is zero. In graph theory, a _____ is the fundamental unit out of which graphs are formed

Chapter 7. Roots, Radicals, and Complex Numbers

    a. Vertex0
    c. Undefined
    b. Thing
    d. Undefined

125. In mathematics, the _____ of two sets A and B is the set that contains all elements of A that also belong to B (or equivalently, all elements of B that also belong to A), but no other elements.
    a. Thing
    b. Intersection0
    c. Undefined
    d. Undefined

126. A _____ is an instrument used in geometry technical drawing and engineering/building to measure distances and/or to rule straight lines.
    a. Ruler0
    b. Thing
    c. Undefined
    d. Undefined

127. In mathematics, the _____ i (or sometimes the Latin j or the Greek iota, see below) allows the real number system R to be extended to the complex number system C. Its precise definition is dependent upon the particular method of extension.
    a. Thing
    b. Imaginary unit0
    c. Undefined
    d. Undefined

128. In mathematics, the _____ of a complex number z, is the first element of the ordered pair of real numbers representing z, i.e. if z = (x,y), or equivalently, z = x + iy, then the _____ of z is x. It is denoted by Re{z} . The complex function which maps z to the _____ of z is not holomorphic.
    a. Real part0
    b. Thing
    c. Undefined
    d. Undefined

129. In mathematics, the _____ of a complex number z, is the second element of the ordered pair of real numbers representing z, i.e. if z = (x,y), or equivalently, z = x + iy, then the _____ of z is y.
    a. Thing
    b. Imaginary part0
    c. Undefined
    d. Undefined

130. In mathematics, a _____ is an expression that is constructed from one or more variables and constants, using only the operations of addition, subtraction, multiplication, and constant positive whole number exponents. is a _____. Note in particular that division by an expression containing a variable is not in general allowed in polynomials. [1]
    a. Polynomial0
    b. Thing
    c. Undefined
    d. Undefined

131. Electrical _____, or simply _____, is a term coined by Oliver Heaviside in July of 1886 to describe a measure of opposition to a sinusoidal alternating current.
    a. Impedance0
    b. Thing
    c. Undefined
    d. Undefined

132. The plus and _____ signs are mathematical symbols used to represent the notions of positive and negative as well as the operations of addition and subtraction.
    a. Minus0
    b. Thing
    c. Undefined
    d. Undefined

Chapter 7. Roots, Radicals, and Complex Numbers

133. In chemistry, a _____ is substance made by combining two or more different materials in such a way that no chemical reaction occurs.
   a. Mixture0
   b. Thing
   c. Undefined
   d. Undefined

134. _____ is the distance around a given two-dimensional object. As a general rule, the _____ of a polygon can always be calculated by adding all the length of the sides together. So, the formula for triangles is P = a + b + c, where a, b and c stand for each side of it. For quadrilaterals the equation is P = a + b + c + d. For equilateral polygons, P = na, where n is the number of sides and a is the side length.
   a. Thing
   b. Perimeter0
   c. Undefined
   d. Undefined

135. In geometry, a _____ is defined as a quadrilateral where all four of its angles are right angles.
   a. Thing
   b. Rectangle0
   c. Undefined
   d. Undefined

136. The _____ in a vacuum is an important physical constant denoted by the letter c for constant or the Latin word celeritas meaning "swiftness
   a. Speed of light0
   b. Thing
   c. Undefined
   d. Undefined

137. _____ is electromagnetic radiation with a wavelength that is visible to the eye (visible _____) or, in a technical or scientific context, electromagnetic radiation of any wavelength.
   a. Thing
   b. Light0
   c. Undefined
   d. Undefined

138. In physics, a _____ may refer to the scalar _____ or to the vector _____.
   a. Potential0
   b. Thing
   c. Undefined
   d. Undefined

139. The _____ of an object is the extra energy which it possesses due to its motion.
   a. Thing
   b. Kinetic energy0
   c. Undefined
   d. Undefined

140. _____ is the SI unit of energy.
   a. Joule0
   b. Thing
   c. Undefined
   d. Undefined

141. The _____ or kilogramme is the SI base unit of mass. It is defined as being equal to the mass of the international prototype of the _____.
   a. Thing
   b. Kilogram0
   c. Undefined
   d. Undefined

142. _____ are flexible, elastic objects used to store mechanical energy.

Chapter 7. Roots, Radicals, and Complex Numbers

a. Thing
b. Springs0
c. Undefined
d. Undefined

143. A _____ is a set of possible values that a variable can take on in order to satisfy a given set of conditions, which may include equations and inequalities.
a. Thing
b. Solution set0
c. Undefined
d. Undefined

144. _____ are the basic objects of study in graph theory. Informally speaking, a graph is a set of objects called points, nodes, or vertices connected by links called lines or edges.
a. Thing
b. Graphs0
c. Undefined
d. Undefined

145. The existence and properties of _____ are the basis of Euclid's parallel postulate. _____ are two lines on the same plane that do not intersect even assuming that lines extend to infinity in either direction.
a. Thing
b. Parallel lines0
c. Undefined
d. Undefined

146. In geometry, two lines or planes if one falls on the other in such a way as to create congruent adjacent angles. The term may be used as a noun or adjective. Thus, referring to Figure 1, the line AB is the _____ to CD through the point B.
a. Perpendicular0
b. Thing
c. Undefined
d. Undefined

147. In algebra, a _____ is a function depending on n that associates a scalar, det(A), to every $n \times n$ square matrix A.
a. Thing
b. Determinant0
c. Undefined
d. Undefined

148. In mathematics, two quantities are called _____ if they vary in such a way that one of the quantities is a constant multiple of the other, or equivalently if they have a constant ratio.
a. Thing
b. Proportional0
c. Undefined
d. Undefined

Chapter 8. Quadratic Functions

1. In mathematics, a _____ is a polynomial equation of the second degree. The general form is $ax^2 + bx + c = 0$.
   a. Quadratic equation0
   b. Thing
   c. Undefined
   d. Undefined

2. A _____ is a symbolic representation denoting a quantity or expression. It often represents an "unknown" quantity that has the potential to change.
   a. Thing
   b. Variable0
   c. Undefined
   d. Undefined

3. _____ systems represent systems whose behavior is not expressible as a sum of the behaviors of its descriptors.
   a. Thing
   b. Nonlinear0
   c. Undefined
   d. Undefined

4. In mathematics, an _____ is a statement about the relative size or order of two objects.
   a. Inequality0
   b. Thing
   c. Undefined
   d. Undefined

5. In plane geometry, a _____ is a polygon with four equal sides, four right angles, and parallel opposite sides. In algebra, the _____ of a number is that number multiplied by itself.
   a. Square0
   b. Thing
   c. Undefined
   d. Undefined

6. In mathematics, a _____ of a number x is a number r such that $r^2 = x$, or in words, a number r whose square (the result of multiplying the number by itself) is x.
   a. Square root0
   b. Thing
   c. Undefined
   d. Undefined

7. In mathematics, a _____ of a complex-valued function f is a member x of the domain of f such that f(x) vanishes at x, that is, x : f (x) = 0.
   a. Root0
   b. Thing
   c. Undefined
   d. Undefined

8. _____ is a technique used in algebra to solve quadratic equations, in analytic geometry for determining the shapes of graphs, and in calculus for computing integrals, including, but hardly limited to, the integrals that define Laplace transforms. The essential objective is to reduce a quadratic polynomial in a variable in an equation or expression to a squared polynomial of linear order. This can reduce an equation or integral to one that is more easily solved or evaluated.
   a. Completing the square0
   b. Thing
   c. Undefined
   d. Undefined

9. In mathematics, _____ is the decomposition of an object into a product of other objects, or factors, which when multiplied together give the original.
   a. Factoring0
   b. Thing
   c. Undefined
   d. Undefined

10. A quadratic equation with real solutions, called roots, which may be real or complex, is given by the _____: $x = {-b \pm \sqrt{b^2 - 4ac}}/{}$

Chapter 8. Quadratic Functions 113

a. Quadratic formula0
b. Thing
c. Undefined
d. Undefined

11. The plus and _____ signs are mathematical symbols used to represent the notions of positive and negative as well as the operations of addition and subtraction.
    a. Thing
    b. Minus0
    c. Undefined
    d. Undefined

12. A _____ is a negotiable instrument instructing a financial institution to pay a specific amount of a specific currency from a specific demand account held in the maker/depositor's name with that institution. Both the maker and payee may be natural persons or legal entities.
    a. Thing
    b. Check0
    c. Undefined
    d. Undefined

13. The _____, the average in everyday English, which is also called the arithmetic _____ (and is distinguished from the geometric _____ or harmonic _____). The average is also called the sample _____. The expected value of a random variable, which is also called the population _____.
    a. Thing
    b. Mean0
    c. Undefined
    d. Undefined

14. In mathematics, a _____ may be described informally as a number that can be given by an infinite decimal representation.
    a. Real number0
    b. Thing
    c. Undefined
    d. Undefined

15. A _____ is a polynomial consisting of three terms; in other words, it is the sum of three monomials.
    a. Thing
    b. Trinomial0
    c. Undefined
    d. Undefined

16. The term _____ can refer to an integer which is the square of some other integer, or an algebraic expression that can be factored as the square of some other expression.
    a. Perfect square0
    b. Thing
    c. Undefined
    d. Undefined

17. In elementary algebra, a _____ is a polynomial with two terms: the sum of two monomials. It is the simplest kind of polynomial except for a monomial.
    a. Binomial0
    b. Thing
    c. Undefined
    d. Undefined

18. In mathematics, a _____ is a constant multiplicative factor of a certain object. The object can be such things as a variable, a vector, a function, etc. For example, the _____ of $9x^2$ is 9.
    a. Thing
    b. Coefficient0
    c. Undefined
    d. Undefined

19. In mathematics and the mathematical sciences, a _____ is a fixed, but possibly unspecified, value. This is in contrast to a variable, which is not fixed.

a. Thing
c. Undefined
b. Constant0
d. Undefined

20. _____ is a fixed, but possibly unspecified, value. This is in contrast to a variable, which is not fixed.
a. Constant term0
c. Undefined
b. Thing
d. Undefined

21. In mathematics, there are several meanings of _____ depending on the subject.
a. Degree0
c. Undefined
b. Thing
d. Undefined

22. In mathematics, _____ is an elementary arithmetic operation. When one of the numbers is a whole number, _____ is the repeated sum of the other number.
a. Multiplication0
c. Undefined
b. Thing
d. Undefined

23. Two mathematical objects are equal if and only if they are precisely the same in every way. This defines a binary relation, _____, denoted by the sign of _____ "=" in such a way that the statement "x = y" means that x and y are equal.
a. Thing
c. Undefined
b. Equality0
d. Undefined

24. An _____ is a combination of numbers, operators, grouping symbols and/or free variables and bound variables arranged in a meaningful way which can be evaluated..
a. Expression0
c. Undefined
b. Thing
d. Undefined

25. In mathematics, a _____ is the result of multiplying, or an expression that identifies factors to be multiplied.
a. Thing
c. Undefined
b. Product0
d. Undefined

26. A _____ is a special kind of ratio, indicating a relationship between two measurements with different units, such as miles to gallons or cents to pounds.
a. Thing
c. Undefined
b. Rate0
d. Undefined

27. _____ is a kind of property which exists as magnitude or multitude. It is among the basic classes of things along with quality, substance, change, and relation.
a. Thing
c. Undefined
b. Amount0
d. Undefined

28. _____ is the fee paid on borrowed money.
a. Thing
c. Undefined
b. Interest0
d. Undefined

Chapter 8. Quadratic Functions

29. A _____ are accounts maintained by commercial banks, savings and loan associations, credit unions, and mutual savings banks that pay interest but can not be used directly as money by, for example, writing a cheque.
 a. Savings account0 b. Thing
 c. Undefined d. Undefined

30. In banking and accountancy, the outstanding _____ is the amount of money owned, or due, that remains in a deposit account or a loan account at a given date, after all past remittances, payments and withdrawal have been accounted for.
 a. Thing b. Balance0
 c. Undefined d. Undefined

31. An _____ is the fee paid on borrow money.
 a. Concept b. Interest rate0
 c. Undefined d. Undefined

32. In geometry, a _____ is defined as a quadrilateral where all four of its angles are right angles.
 a. Rectangle0 b. Thing
 c. Undefined d. Undefined

33. A _____ is a unit of length, usually used to measure distance, in a number of different systems, including Imperial units, United States customary units and Norwegian/Swedish mil. Its size can vary from system to system, but in each is between 1 and 10 kilometers. In contemporary English contexts _____ refers to either:
 a. Mile0 b. Thing
 c. Undefined d. Undefined

34. _____ is a unit of speed, expressing the number of international miles covered per hour.
 a. Miles per hour0 b. Thing
 c. Undefined d. Undefined

35. The _____ are the only integral domain whose positive elements are well-ordered, and in which order is preserved by addition. Like the natural numbers, the _____ form a countably infinite set. The set of all _____ is usually denoted in mathematics by a boldface Z .
 a. Thing b. Integers0
 c. Undefined d. Undefined

36. _____ means in succession or back-to-back
 a. Consecutive0 b. Thing
 c. Undefined d. Undefined

37. In Euclidean geometry, a _____ is the set of all points in a plane at a fixed distance, called the radius, from a given point, the center.
 a. Thing b. Circle0
 c. Undefined d. Undefined

38. A _____ can refer to a line joining two nonadjacent vertices of a polygon or polyhedron, or in some contexts any upward or downward sloping line. .

a. Diagonal0
b. Thing
c. Undefined
d. Undefined

39. A _____ is one of the basic shapes of geometry: a polygon with three vertices and three sides which are straight line segments.
   a. Thing
   b. Triangle0
   c. Undefined
   d. Undefined

40. _____ has one 90° internal angle a right angle.
   a. Thing
   b. Right triangle0
   c. Undefined
   d. Undefined

41. In geometry, a _____ (Greek words diairo = divide and metro = measure) of a circle is any straight line segment that passes through the centre and whose endpoints are on the circular boundary, or, in more modern usage, the length of such a line segment. When using the word in the more modern sense, one speaks of the _____ rather than a _____, because all diameters of a circle have the same length. This length is twice the radius. The _____ of a circle is also the longest chord that the circle has.
   a. Thing
   b. Diameter0
   c. Undefined
   d. Undefined

42. In classical geometry, a _____ of a circle or sphere is any line segment from its center to its boundary. By extension, the _____ of a circle or sphere is the length of any such segment. The _____ is half the diameter. In science and engineering the term _____ of curvature is commonly used as a synonym for _____.
   a. Thing
   b. Radius0
   c. Undefined
   d. Undefined

43. An _____ triange is a triangle with at least two sides of equal length.
   a. Isosceles0
   b. Thing
   c. Undefined
   d. Undefined

44. The metre (or _____, see spelling differences) is a measure of length. It is the basic unit of length in the metric system and in the International System of Units (SI), used around the world for general and scientific purposes.
   a. Meter0
   b. Concept
   c. Undefined
   d. Undefined

45. The _____ of a solid object is the three-dimensional concept of how much space it occupies, often quantified numerically.
   a. Thing
   b. Volume0
   c. Undefined
   d. Undefined

46. In mathematics, a _____ is a quadric surface, with the following equation in Cartesian coordinates: $(x/_a)^2 + (y/_b)^2 = 1$.
   a. Cylinder0
   b. Thing
   c. Undefined
   d. Undefined

Chapter 8. Quadratic Functions

47. _____ of a polynomial with real or complex coefficients is a certain expression in the coefficients of the polynomial which is equal to zero if and only if the polynomial has a multiple root i.e. a root with multiplicity greater than one in the complex numbers.
   a. Thing
   b. Discriminant0
   c. Undefined
   d. Undefined

48. In geometry, the _____ of an object is a point in some sense in the middle of the object.
   a. Thing
   b. Center0
   c. Undefined
   d. Undefined

49. _____ is a notation for writing numbers that is often used by scientists and mathematicians to make it easier to write large and small numbers.
   a. Scientific notation0
   b. Thing
   c. Undefined
   d. Undefined

50. In mathematics, a _____ is the end result of a division problem. It can also be expressed as the number of times the divisor divides into the dividend.
   a. Quotient0
   b. Thing
   c. Undefined
   d. Undefined

51. The _____ is a method of finding the derivative of a function that is the quotient of two other functions for which derivatives exist.
   a. Quotient rule0
   b. Thing
   c. Undefined
   d. Undefined

52. A _____ is the part of a fraction that tells how many equal parts make up a whole, and which is used in the name of the fraction: "halves", "thirds", "fourths" or "quarters", "fifths" and so on.
   a. Denominator0
   b. Concept
   c. Undefined
   d. Undefined

53. A _____ is a deliberate process for transforming one or more inputs into one or more results.
   a. Thing
   b. Calculation0
   c. Undefined
   d. Undefined

54. In mathematics, _____ expressions is used to reduce the expression into the lowest possible term.
   a. Thing
   b. Simplifying0
   c. Undefined
   d. Undefined

55. A _____ is a numeral used to indicate a count. The most common use of the word today is to name the part of a fraction that tells the number or count of equal parts.
   a. Thing
   b. Numerator0
   c. Undefined
   d. Undefined

56. _____ is the largest positive integer that divides both numbers without remainder.

Chapter 8. Quadratic Functions

    a. Common Factor0   b. Thing
    c. Undefined   d. Undefined

57. A _____ is a polynomial function of the form $f(x) = ax^2 + bx + c$, where a, b, c are real numbers and a , 0.
    a. Event   b. Quadratic function0
    c. Undefined   d. Undefined

58. The mathematical concept of a _____ expresses the intuitive idea of deterministic dependence between two quantities, one of which is viewed as primary and the other as secondary. A _____ then is a way to associate a unique output for each input of a specified type, for example, a real number or an element of a given set.
    a. Function0   b. Thing
    c. Undefined   d. Undefined

59. _____ are the basic objects of study in graph theory. Informally speaking, a graph is a set of objects called points, nodes, or vertices connected by links called lines or edges.
    a. Graphs0   b. Thing
    c. Undefined   d. Undefined

60. _____ is a business term for the amount of money that a company receives from its activities in a given period, mostly from sales of products and/or services to customers
    a. Revenue0   b. Thing
    c. Undefined   d. Undefined

61. _____, Greek for "knowledge of nature," is the branch of science concerned with the discovery and characterization of universal laws which govern matter, energy, space, and time.
    a. Thing   b. Physics0
    c. Undefined   d. Undefined

62. _____ of an object is its speed in a particular direction.
    a. Thing   b. Velocity0
    c. Undefined   d. Undefined

63. Initial objects are also called _____, and terminal objects are also called final.
    a. Thing   b. Coterminal0
    c. Undefined   d. Undefined

64. _____ is defined as the rate of change or derivative with respect to time of velocity.
    a. Acceleration0   b. Thing
    c. Undefined   d. Undefined

65. A _____ is a simplified and structured visual representation of concepts, ideas, constructions, relations, statistical data, anatomy etc used in all aspects of human activities to visualize and clarify the topic.
    a. Thing   b. Diagram0
    c. Undefined   d. Undefined

Chapter 8. Quadratic Functions

66. _____ forms part of thinking. Considered the most complex of all intellectual functions, _____ has been defined as higher-order cognitive process that requires the modulation and control of more routine or fundamental skills.
  a. Thing
  b. Problem solving0
  c. Undefined
  d. Undefined

67. In mathematics, an _____ number is any real number that is not a rational number- that is, it is a number which cannot be expressed as a fraction m/n, where m and n are integers.
  a. Thing
  b. Irrational0
  c. Undefined
  d. Undefined

68. In mathematics, an _____ is any real number that is not a rational number ¡ª that is, it is a number which cannot be expressed as m/n, where m and n are integers.
  a. Irrational number0
  b. Thing
  c. Undefined
  d. Undefined

69. In mathematics, _____ are any real number that is not a rational number ¡ª that is, it is a number which cannot be expressed as m/n, where m and n are integers.
  a. Irrational numbers0
  b. Thing
  c. Undefined
  d. Undefined

70. A _____ is a three-dimensional solid object bounded by six square faces, facets, or sides, with three meeting at each vertex.
  a. Thing
  b. Cube0
  c. Undefined
  d. Undefined

71. _____, from Latin meaning "to make progress", is defined in two different ways. Pure economic _____ is the increase in wealth that an investor has from making an investment, taking into consideration all costs associated with that investment including the opportunity cost of capital.
  a. Profit0
  b. Thing
  c. Undefined
  d. Undefined

72. In mathematics, an _____, mean, or central tendency of a data set refers to a measure of the "middle" or "expected" value of the data set.
  a. Average0
  b. Concept
  c. Undefined
  d. Undefined

73. _____ is a statistical measure of the average length of survival of a living thing.
  a. Thing
  b. Life expectancy0
  c. Undefined
  d. Undefined

74. In mathematics, a matrix can be thought of as each row or _____ being a vector. Hence, a space formed by row vectors or _____ vectors are said to be a row space or a _____ space.
  a. Column0
  b. Concept
  c. Undefined
  d. Undefined

Chapter 8. Quadratic Functions

75. The _____ of a function is an extension of the concept of a sum, and are identified or found through the use of integration.
    a. Integral0
    b. Thing
    c. Undefined
    d. Undefined

76. In mathematics and more specifically set theory, the _____ set is the unique set which contains no elements.
    a. Empty0
    b. Thing
    c. Undefined
    d. Undefined

77. _____ is a three-dimensional geometric shape formed by straight lines through a fixed point vertex to the points of a fixed curve directrix.
    a. Right circular cone0
    b. Thing
    c. Undefined
    d. Undefined

78. A _____ is a three-dimensional geometric shape formed by straight lines through a fixed point (vertex) to the points of a fixed curve (directrix)
    a. Cone0
    b. Concept
    c. Undefined
    d. Undefined

79. _____ is a temperature scale named after the German physicist Daniel Gabriel _____ , who proposed it in 1724.
    a. Fahrenheit0
    b. Thing
    c. Undefined
    d. Undefined

80. _____ is a physical property of a system that underlies the common notions of hot and cold; something that is hotter has the greater _____.
    a. Thing
    b. Temperature0
    c. Undefined
    d. Undefined

81. _____ are a measure of time.
    a. Minutes0
    b. Thing
    c. Undefined
    d. Undefined

82. _____ is a way of expressing a number as a fraction of 100 per cent meaning "per hundred".
    a. Percent0
    b. Thing
    c. Undefined
    d. Undefined

83. _____ is the transport of people on a trip/journey or the process or time involved in a person or object moving from one location to another.
    a. Travel0
    b. Thing
    c. Undefined
    d. Undefined

84. _____ are flexible, elastic objects used to store mechanical energy.
    a. Springs0
    b. Thing
    c. Undefined
    d. Undefined

Chapter 8. Quadratic Functions

85. The State of _____ is a state located in the Rocky Mountain region of the United States of America.
    a. Colorado0
    b. Thing
    c. Undefined
    d. Undefined

86. In mathematics, a _____ is a two-dimensional manifold or surface that is perfectly flat.
    a. Thing
    b. Plane0
    c. Undefined
    d. Undefined

87. _____ is a state located in the southern and southwestern regions of the United States of America.
    a. Thing
    b. Texas0
    c. Undefined
    d. Undefined

88. In mathematics, a _____ is a homogeneous polynomial of degree two in a number of variables.
    a. Thing
    b. Quadratic form0
    c. Undefined
    d. Undefined

89. _____ is a mathematical operation, written a^n, involving two numbers, the base a and the exponent n.
    a. Exponentiating0
    b. Thing
    c. Undefined
    d. Undefined

90. _____ is a mathematical operation, written a^n, involving two numbers, the base a and the exponent n.
    a. Thing
    b. Exponentiation0
    c. Undefined
    d. Undefined

91. In mathematics, a _____ is an expression that is constructed from one or more variables and constants, using only the operations of addition, subtraction, multiplication, and constant positive whole number exponents. is a _____. Note in particular that division by an expression containing a variable is not in general allowed in polynomials. [1]
    a. Thing
    b. Polynomial0
    c. Undefined
    d. Undefined

92. _____ variables are variables other than the independent variable that may bear any effect on the behavior of the subject being studied.
    a. Thing
    b. Extraneous0
    c. Undefined
    d. Undefined

93. In mathematics, a _____ number is a number which can be expressed as a ratio of two integers. Non-integer _____ numbers (commonly called fractions) are usually written as the vulgar fraction a / b, where b is not zero.
    a. Rational0
    b. Thing
    c. Undefined
    d. Undefined

94. _____ has many meanings, most of which simply .
    a. Thing
    b. Power0
    c. Undefined
    d. Undefined

95. _____ is the symbol used to indicate the nth root of a number

a. Thing
b. Radical0
c. Undefined
d. Undefined

96. In geometry, a _____ is a special kind of point, usually a corner of a polygon, polyhedron, or higher dimensional polytope. In the geometry of curves a _____ is a point of where the first derivative of curvature is zero. In graph theory, a _____ is the fundamental unit out of which graphs are formed
   a. Vertex0
   b. Thing
   c. Undefined
   d. Undefined

97. _____ means "constancy", i.e. if something retains a certain feature even after we change a way of looking at it, then it is symmetric.
   a. Symmetry0
   b. Thing
   c. Undefined
   d. Undefined

98. An _____ is a straight line around which a geometric figure can be rotated.
   a. Axis0
   b. Thing
   c. Undefined
   d. Undefined

99. _____ of a two-dimensional figure is a line such that, if a perpendicular is constructed, any two points lying on the perpendicular at equal distances from the _____ are identical.
   a. Thing
   b. Axis of symmetry0
   c. Undefined
   d. Undefined

100. In mathematics, the _____ is a conic section generated by the intersection of a right circular conical surface and a plane parallel to a generating straight line of that surface. It can also be defined as locus of points in a plane which are equidistant from a given point.
   a. Thing
   b. Parabola0
   c. Undefined
   d. Undefined

101. Any point where a graph makes contact with an coordinate axis is called an _____ of the graph
   a. Intercept0
   b. Thing
   c. Undefined
   d. Undefined

102. In Euclidean geometry, a _____ is moving every point a constant distance in a specified direction.
   a. Translation0
   b. Concept
   c. Undefined
   d. Undefined

103. In mathematics, the concept of a _____ tries to capture the intuitive idea of a geometrical one-dimensional and continuous object. A simple example is the circle.
   a. Thing
   b. Curve0
   c. Undefined
   d. Undefined

104. A _____ is a set of numbers that designate location in a given reference system, such as x,y in a planar _____ system or an x,y,z in a three-dimensional _____ system.

Chapter 8. Quadratic Functions

a. Coordinate0
b. Thing
c. Undefined
d. Undefined

105. _____, either of the curved-bracket punctuation marks that together make a set of _____
a. Parentheses0
b. Thing
c. Undefined
d. Undefined

106. An _____ is a collection of two not necessarily distinct objects, one of which is distinguished as the first coordinate and the other as the second coordinate.
a. Ordered pair0
b. Thing
c. Undefined
d. Undefined

107. In mathematics, an inequality is a statement about the relative size or order of two objects. For example 14 > 10, or 14 is _____ 10.
a. Greater than0
b. Thing
c. Undefined
d. Undefined

108. The _____ of measurement are a globally standardized and modernized form of the metric system.
a. Thing
b. Units0
c. Undefined
d. Undefined

109. _____ is the distance around a given two-dimensional object. As a general rule, the _____ of a polygon can always be calculated by adding all the length of the sides together. So, the formula for triangles is P = a + b + c, where a, b and c stand for each side of it. For quadrilaterals the equation is P = a + b + c + d. For equilateral polygons, P = na, where n is the number of sides and a is the side length.
a. Thing
b. Perimeter0
c. Undefined
d. Undefined

110. A frame of _____ is a particular perspective from which the universe is observed.
a. Thing
b. Reference0
c. Undefined
d. Undefined

111. In astronomy, geography, geometry and related sciences and contexts, a plane is said to be _____ at a given point if it is locally perpendicular to the gradient of the gravity field, i.e., with the direction of the gravitational force at that point.
a. Thing
b. Horizontal0
c. Undefined
d. Undefined

112. _____ is a set, with some particular properties and usually some additional structure, such as the operations of addition or multiplication, for instance.
a. Space0
b. Thing
c. Undefined
d. Undefined

113. Sound is a disturbance of mechanical energy that propagates through matter as a wave or _____.
a. Sound wave0
b. Thing
c. Undefined
d. Undefined

Chapter 8. Quadratic Functions

114. The existence and properties of _____ are the basis of Euclid's parallel postulate. _____ are two lines on the same plane that do not intersect even assuming that lines extend to infinity in either direction.
 a. Parallel lines0
 b. Thing
 c. Undefined
 d. Undefined

115. _____ is electromagnetic radiation with a wavelength that is visible to the eye (visible _____) or, in a technical or scientific context, electromagnetic radiation of any wavelength.
 a. Thing
 b. Light0
 c. Undefined
 d. Undefined

116. In mathematics, _____ are the intuitive idea of a geometrical one-dimensional and continuous object.
 a. Thing
 b. Curves0
 c. Undefined
 d. Undefined

117. Equivalence is the condition of being _____ or essentially equal.
 a. Equivalent0
 b. Thing
 c. Undefined
 d. Undefined

118. The population _____ is the total number of human beings alive on the planet Earth at a given time.
 a. Thing
 b. Of the world0
 c. Undefined
 d. Undefined

119. In business, particularly accounting, a _____ is the time intervals that the accounts, statement, payments, or other calculations cover.
 a. Period0
 b. Thing
 c. Undefined
 d. Undefined

120. In mathematics, a _____ is a countable collection of open covers of a topological space that satisfies certain separation axioms.
 a. Development0
 b. Thing
 c. Undefined
 d. Undefined

121. _____ are activities that are governed by a set of rules or customs and often engaged in competitively.
 a. Thing
 b. Sports0
 c. Undefined
 d. Undefined

122. In algebra, a _____ is a function depending on *n* that associates a scalar, det(*A*), to every *n*×*n* square matrix *A*.
 a. Determinant0
 b. Thing
 c. Undefined
 d. Undefined

123. The word _____ comes from the Latin word linearis, which means created by lines.
 a. Thing
 b. Linear0
 c. Undefined
 d. Undefined

124. A _____ is a one-dimensional picture in which the integers are shown as specially-marked points evenly spaced on a line.

Chapter 8. Quadratic Functions

a. Thing
b. Number line0
c. Undefined
d. Undefined

125. Mathematical _____ is used to represent ideas.
a. Notation0
b. Thing
c. Undefined
d. Undefined

126. In elementary algebra, an _____ is a set that contains every real number between two indicated numbers and may contain the two numbers themselves.
a. Thing
b. Interval0
c. Undefined
d. Undefined

127. _____ is the notation in which permitted values for a variable are expressed as ranging over a certain interval; "5 < x < 9" is an example of the application of _____.
a. Thing
b. Interval notation0
c. Undefined
d. Undefined

128. A _____ is a set of possible values that a variable can take on in order to satisfy a given set of conditions, which may include equations and inequalities.
a. Solution set0
b. Thing
c. Undefined
d. Undefined

129. Acid _____ ratio measures the ability of a company to use its near cash or quick assets to immediately extinguish its current liabilities.
a. Test0
b. Thing
c. Undefined
d. Undefined

130. In common philosophical language, a proposition or _____, is the content of an assertion, that is, it is true-or-false and defined by the meaning of a particular piece of language.
a. Concept
b. Statement0
c. Undefined
d. Undefined

131. In mathematics, factorization (British English: factorisation) or factoring is the decomposition of an object (for example, a number, a polynomial, or a matrix) into a product of other objects, or _____, which when multiplied together give the original.
a. Thing
b. Factors0
c. Undefined
d. Undefined

132. In topology, the _____ are subsets S of a topological space X is the set of points which can be approached both from S and from the outside of S.
a. Thing
b. Boundaries0
c. Undefined
d. Undefined

133. In abstract algebra, _____ consists of sets with binary operations that satisfy certain axioms.

a. Thing
c. Undefined
b. Grouping0
d. Undefined

134. _____ is, or relates to, the _____ temperature scale .
    a. Celsius0
    b. Thing
    c. Undefined
    d. Undefined

135. _____ is a relation in Euclidean geometry among the three sides of a right triangle.
    a. Thing
    b. Pythagorean Theorem0
    c. Undefined
    d. Undefined

136. In physics and in _____ calculus, a spatial _____, or simply _____, is a concept characterized by a magnitude and a direction.
    a. Vector0
    b. Thing
    c. Undefined
    d. Undefined

137. In mathematics, a _____ is a statement that can be proved on the basis of explicitly stated or previously agreed assumptions.
    a. Thing
    b. Theorem0
    c. Undefined
    d. Undefined

138. _____ is often used to describe the measurement of the steepness, incline, gradient, or grade of a straight line. The _____ is defined as the ratio of the "rise" divided by the "run" between two points on a line, or in other words, the ratio of the altitude change to the horizontal distance between any two points on the line.
    a. Slope0
    b. Thing
    c. Undefined
    d. Undefined

139. In mathematics, the _____ of a function is the set of all "output" values produced by that function. Given a function $f : A \to B$, the _____ of f, is defined to be the set $\{x \in B : x = f(a) \text{ for some } a \in A\}$.
    a. Range0
    b. Thing
    c. Undefined
    d. Undefined

140. In mathematics, a _____ of a k-place relation $L \subseteq X_1 \times \ldots \times X_k$ is one of the sets X_j, $1 \leq j \leq k$. In the special case where k = 2 and $L \subseteq X_1 \times X_2$ is a function $L : X_1 \to X_2$, it is conventional to refer to X_1 as the _____ of the function and to refer to X_2 as the codomain of the function.
    a. Domain0
    b. Thing
    c. Undefined
    d. Undefined

141. _____ is electric power as defined as the amount of work done by an electric current, or the rate at which electrical energy is transferred.
    a. Thing
    b. Wattage0
    c. Undefined
    d. Undefined

142. The _____, in practice often shortened to amp, is a unit of electric current, or amount of electric charge per second.

Chapter 8. Quadratic Functions

a. Amperes0
b. Thing
c. Undefined
d. Undefined

143. The _____ is the total number of human beings alive on the planet Earth at a given time.
   a. World population0
   b. Thing
   c. Undefined
   d. Undefined

144. In sociology and biology a _____ is the collection of people or organisms of a particular species living in a given geographic area or space, usually measured by a census.
   a. Population0
   b. Thing
   c. Undefined
   d. Undefined

145. In mathematics, _____ growth occurs when the growth rate of a function is always proportional to the function's current size.
   a. Exponential0
   b. Thing
   c. Undefined
   d. Undefined

146. _____ is one of the most important functions in mathematics. A function commonly used to study growth and decay
   a. Thing
   b. Exponential function0
   c. Undefined
   d. Undefined

Chapter 9. Exponential and Logarithmic Functions

1. A _____ number is a positive integer which has a positive divisor other than one or itself.
   a. Thing
   b. Composite0
   c. Undefined
   d. Undefined

2. The mathematical concept of a _____ expresses the intuitive idea of deterministic dependence between two quantities, one of which is viewed as primary and the other as secondary. A _____ then is a way to associate a unique output for each input of a specified type, for example, a real number or an element of a given set.
   a. Function0
   b. Thing
   c. Undefined
   d. Undefined

3. _____ element of an element x with respect to a binary operation * with identity element e is an element y such that x * y = y * x = e. In particular,
   a. Thing
   b. Inverse0
   c. Undefined
   d. Undefined

4. An _____ is a function which does the reverse of a given function.
   a. Inverse function0
   b. Thing
   c. Undefined
   d. Undefined

5. _____ is the process in which an unstable atomic nucleus loses energy by emitting radiation in the form of particles or electromagnetic waves.
   a. Thing
   b. Radioactive decay0
   c. Undefined
   d. Undefined

6. _____ is a radiometric dating method that uses the naturally occurring isotope carbon-14 to determine the age of carbonaceous materials up to about 60,000 years.
   a. Radiocarbon dating0
   b. Thing
   c. Undefined
   d. Undefined

7. In mathematics, _____ growth occurs when the growth rate of a function is always proportional to the function's current size.
   a. Exponential0
   b. Thing
   c. Undefined
   d. Undefined

8. _____ is one of the most important functions in mathematics. A function commonly used to study growth and decay
   a. Exponential function0
   b. Thing
   c. Undefined
   d. Undefined

9. _____ is the fee paid on borrowed money.
   a. Interest0
   b. Thing
   c. Undefined
   d. Undefined

10. In mathematics, an _____ number is any real number that is not a rational number- that is, it is a number which cannot be expressed as a fraction m/n, where m and n are integers.

Chapter 9. Exponential and Logarithmic Functions

    a. Thing
    c. Undefined
    b. Irrational0
    d. Undefined

11. In mathematics, an _____ is any real number that is not a rational number ¡ª that is, it is a number which cannot be expressed as m/n, where m and n are integers.
    a. Irrational number0
    c. Undefined
    b. Thing
    d. Undefined

12. In mathematics, a _____ of a positive integer n is a way of writing n as a sum of positive integers.
    a. Composition0
    c. Undefined
    b. Thing
    d. Undefined

13. A _____ is a symbolic representation denoting a quantity or expression. It often represents an "unknown" quantity that has the potential to change.
    a. Thing
    c. Undefined
    b. Variable0
    d. Undefined

14. A _____, formed by the composition of one function on another, represents the application of the former to the result of the application of the latter to the argument of the composite.
    a. Composite function0
    c. Undefined
    b. Thing
    d. Undefined

15. A _____ is 360° or 2π radians.
    a. Thing
    c. Undefined
    b. Turn0
    d. Undefined

16. In mathematics, a _____ may be described informally as a number that can be given by an infinite decimal representation.
    a. Thing
    c. Undefined
    b. Real number0
    d. Undefined

17. In mathematics, a _____ of a k-place relation $L \subseteq X_1 \times ... \times X_k$ is one of the sets X_j, $1 \leq j \leq k$. In the special case where k = 2 and $L \subseteq X_1 \times X_2$ is a function $L : X_1 \rightarrow X_2$, it is conventional to refer to X_1 as the _____ of the function and to refer to X_2 as the codomain of the function.
    a. Thing
    c. Undefined
    b. Domain0
    d. Undefined

18. In mathematics, a _____ is the result of multiplying, or an expression that identifies factors to be multiplied.
    a. Product0
    c. Undefined
    b. Thing
    d. Undefined

19. In Euclidean geometry, a _____ is the set of all points in a plane at a fixed distance, called the radius, from a given point, the center.
    a. Thing
    c. Undefined
    b. Circle0
    d. Undefined

Chapter 9. Exponential and Logarithmic Functions

20. An _____ is a collection of two not necessarily distinct objects, one of which is distinguished as the first coordinate and the other as the second coordinate.
    a. Ordered pair0
    b. Thing
    c. Undefined
    d. Undefined

21. In mathematics, the conjugate _____ or adjoint matrix of an m-by-n matrix A with complex entries is the n-by-m matrix A* obtained from A by taking the transpose and then taking the complex conjugate of each entry.
    a. Pairs0
    b. Thing
    c. Undefined
    d. Undefined

22. In mathematics, the _____ of a function is the set of all "output" values produced by that function. Given a function $f : A \to B$, the _____ of f, is defined to be the set $\{x \in B : x = f(a) \text{ for some } a \in A\}$.
    a. Thing
    b. Range0
    c. Undefined
    d. Undefined

23. _____ is a test to determine if a relation or its graph is a function or not
    a. Thing
    b. Vertical line test0
    c. Undefined
    d. Undefined

24. Acid _____ ratio measures the ability of a company to use its near cash or quick assets to immediately extinguish its current liabilities.
    a. Thing
    b. Test0
    c. Undefined
    d. Undefined

25. In astronomy, geography, geometry and related sciences and contexts, a plane is said to be _____ at a given point if it is locally perpendicular to the gradient of the gravity field, i.e., with the direction of the gravitational force at that point.
    a. Thing
    b. Horizontal0
    c. Undefined
    d. Undefined

26. _____ is a test used to determine if a function is injective, surjective or bijective.
    a. Thing
    b. Horizontal line test0
    c. Undefined
    d. Undefined

27. A _____ is a set of numbers that designate location in a given reference system, such as x,y in a planar _____ system or an x,y,z in a three-dimensional _____ system.
    a. Thing
    b. Coordinate0
    c. Undefined
    d. Undefined

28. An _____ is when two lines intersect somewhere on a plane creating a right angle at intersection
    a. Axes0
    b. Thing
    c. Undefined
    d. Undefined

29. _____ are the basic objects of study in graph theory. Informally speaking, a graph is a set of objects called points, nodes, or vertices connected by links called lines or edges.

Chapter 9. Exponential and Logarithmic Functions

   a. Graphs0
   b. Thing
   c. Undefined
   d. Undefined

30. _____ means "constancy", i.e. if something retains a certain feature even after we change a way of looking at it, then it is symmetric.
   a. Symmetry0
   b. Thing
   c. Undefined
   d. Undefined

31. A _____ is a three-dimensional solid object bounded by six square faces, facets, or sides, with three meeting at each vertex.
   a. Thing
   b. Cube0
   c. Undefined
   d. Undefined

32. A _____ of a number is a number a such that $a^3 = x$.
   a. Thing
   b. Cube root0
   c. Undefined
   d. Undefined

33. In mathematics, a _____ is a polynomial equation of the third degree.
   a. Thing
   b. Cubic equation0
   c. Undefined
   d. Undefined

34. Equivalence is the condition of being _____ or essentially equal.
   a. Thing
   b. Equivalent0
   c. Undefined
   d. Undefined

35. In mathematics, a _____ of a complex-valued function f is a member x of the domain of f such that f(x) vanishes at x, that is, x : f (x) = 0.
   a. Root0
   b. Thing
   c. Undefined
   d. Undefined

36. _____ has many meanings, most of which simply .
   a. Power0
   b. Thing
   c. Undefined
   d. Undefined

37. An _____ is a straight line around which a geometric figure can be rotated.
   a. Thing
   b. Axis0
   c. Undefined
   d. Undefined

38. In plane geometry, a _____ is a polygon with four equal sides, four right angles, and parallel opposite sides. In algebra, the _____ of a number is that number multiplied by itself.
   a. Square0
   b. Thing
   c. Undefined
   d. Undefined

39. In geographic information systems, a _____ comprises an entity with a geographic location, typically determined by points, arcs, or polygons. Carriageways and cadastres exemplify _____ data.

a. Thing
b. Feature0
c. Undefined
d. Undefined

40. In mathematics, the _____ of two sets A and B is the set that contains all elements of A that also belong to B (or equivalently, all elements of B that also belong to A), but no other elements.
a. Intersection0
b. Thing
c. Undefined
d. Undefined

41. A _____ is a unit of length, usually used to measure distance, in a number of different systems, including Imperial units, United States customary units and Norwegian/Swedish mil. Its size can vary from system to system, but in each is between 1 and 10 kilometers. In contemporary English contexts _____ refers to either:
a. Thing
b. Mile0
c. Undefined
d. Undefined

42. _____ is a unit of speed, expressing the number of international miles covered per hour.
a. Thing
b. Miles per hour0
c. Undefined
d. Undefined

43. _____ is a temperature scale named after the German physicist Daniel Gabriel _____ , who proposed it in 1724.
a. Thing
b. Fahrenheit0
c. Undefined
d. Undefined

44. _____ is, or relates to, the _____ temperature scale .
a. Thing
b. Celsius0
c. Undefined
d. Undefined

45. In mathematics, there are several meanings of _____ depending on the subject.
a. Degree0
b. Thing
c. Undefined
d. Undefined

46. In classical geometry, a _____ of a circle or sphere is any line segment from its center to its boundary. By extension, the _____ of a circle or sphere is the length of any such segment. The _____ is half the diameter. In science and engineering the term _____ of curvature is commonly used as a synonym for _____ .
a. Thing
b. Radius0
c. Undefined
d. Undefined

47. In mathematics, the concept of a _____ tries to capture the intuitive idea of a geometrical one-dimensional and continuous object. A simple example is the circle.
a. Thing
b. Curve0
c. Undefined
d. Undefined

48. In mathematics, _____ are the intuitive idea of a geometrical one-dimensional and continuous object.
a. Curves0
b. Thing
c. Undefined
d. Undefined

Chapter 9. Exponential and Logarithmic Functions

49. A _____ is a polynomial function of the form $f(x) = ax^2 + bx + c$, where a, b, c are real numbers and a , 0.
    a. Quadratic function0
    b. Event
    c. Undefined
    d. Undefined

50. In mathematics and the mathematical sciences, a _____ is a fixed, but possibly unspecified, value. This is in contrast to a variable, which is not fixed.
    a. Constant0
    b. Thing
    c. Undefined
    d. Undefined

51. In mathematics, _____ occurs when the growth rate of a function is always proportional to the function's current size.
    a. Exponential growth0
    b. Thing
    c. Undefined
    d. Undefined

52. The word _____ comes from the Latin word linearis, which means created by lines.
    a. Linear0
    b. Thing
    c. Undefined
    d. Undefined

53. The _____ of a ring R is defined to be the smallest positive integer n such that n a = 0, for all a in R.
    a. Characteristic0
    b. Thing
    c. Undefined
    d. Undefined

54. In mathematics, an inequality is a statement about the relative size or order of two objects. For example 14 > 10, or 14 is _____ 10.
    a. Thing
    b. Greater than0
    c. Undefined
    d. Undefined

55. A _____ is a special kind of ratio, indicating a relationship between two measurements with different units, such as miles to gallons or cents to pounds.
    a. Thing
    b. Rate0
    c. Undefined
    d. Undefined

56. In business, particularly accounting, a _____ is the time intervals that the accounts, statement, payments, or other calculations cover.
    a. Thing
    b. Period0
    c. Undefined
    d. Undefined

57. _____ is a kind of property which exists as magnitude or multitude. It is among the basic classes of things along with quality, substance, change, and relation.
    a. Thing
    b. Amount0
    c. Undefined
    d. Undefined

58. An _____ is the fee paid on borrow money.
    a. Concept
    b. Interest rate0
    c. Undefined
    d. Undefined

Chapter 9. Exponential and Logarithmic Functions

59. A _____ is an individual or household that purchases and uses goods and services generated within the economy.
    a. Thing
    b. Consumer0
    c. Undefined
    d. Undefined

60. In Graph theory, a _____ is a digraph with weighted edges.
    a. Network0
    b. Concept
    c. Undefined
    d. Undefined

61. The _____, the average in everyday English, which is also called the arithmetic _____ (and is distinguished from the geometric _____ or harmonic _____). The average is also called the sample _____. The expected value of a random variable, which is also called the population _____.
    a. Thing
    b. Mean0
    c. Undefined
    d. Undefined

62. The _____ of measurement are a globally standardized and modernized form of the metric system.
    a. Thing
    b. Units0
    c. Undefined
    d. Undefined

63. The _____ is the total number of human beings alive on the planet Earth at a given time.
    a. Thing
    b. World population0
    c. Undefined
    d. Undefined

64. In sociology and biology a _____ is the collection of people or organisms of a particular species living in a given geographic area or space, usually measured by a census.
    a. Population0
    b. Thing
    c. Undefined
    d. Undefined

65. The _____ is the period of time required for a quantity to double in size or value.
    a. Doubling time0
    b. Thing
    c. Undefined
    d. Undefined

66. _____ interest refers to the fact that whenever interest is calculated, it is based not only on the original principal, but also on any unpaid interest that has been added to the principal.
    a. Compound0
    b. Thing
    c. Undefined
    d. Undefined

67. _____ refers to the fact that whenever interest is calculated, it is based not only on the original principal, but also on any unpaid interest that has been added to the principal. The more frequently interest is compounded, the faster the balance grows.
    a. Concept
    b. Compound interest0
    c. Undefined
    d. Undefined

68. In geometry, an _____ of a triangle is a straight line through a vertex and perpendicular to (i.e. forming a right angle with) the opposite side or an extension of the opposite side.

Chapter 9. Exponential and Logarithmic Functions 135

   a. Concept
   b. Altitude0
   c. Undefined
   d. Undefined

69. A _____ is a unit of length in the metric system, equal to one thousand metres, the current SI base unit of length
   a. Thing
   b. Kilometer0
   c. Undefined
   d. Undefined

70. A _____ is the result of the addition of a set of numbers. The numbers may be natural numbers, complex numbers, matrices, or still more complicated objects. An infinite _____ is a subtle procedure known as a series.
   a. Thing
   b. Sum0
   c. Undefined
   d. Undefined

71. In mathematics, the _____ (or modulus) of a real number is its numerical value without regard to its sign.
   a. Thing
   b. Absolute value0
   c. Undefined
   d. Undefined

72. In mathematics, a _____ of a number x is the exponent y of the power by such that $x = b^y$. The value used for the base b must be neither 0 nor 1, nor a root of 1 in the case of the extension to complex numbers, and is typically 10, e, or 2.
   a. Thing
   b. Logarithm0
   c. Undefined
   d. Undefined

73. The _____ of a mathematical object is its size: a property by which it can be larger or smaller than other objects of the same kind; in technical terms, an ordering of the class of objects to which it belongs.
   a. Magnitude0
   b. Thing
   c. Undefined
   d. Undefined

74. A _____ is a function that assigns a number to subsets of a given set.
   a. Thing
   b. Measure0
   c. Undefined
   d. Undefined

75. An _____ is the result from the sudden release of stored energy in the Earth's crust that creates seismic waves.
   a. Thing
   b. Earthquake0
   c. Undefined
   d. Undefined

76. In Euclidean geometry, a uniform _____ is a linear transformation that enlargers or diminishes objects, and whose _____ factor is the same in all directions. This is also called homothethy.
   a. Scale0
   b. Thing
   c. Undefined
   d. Undefined

77. The _____ governs the differentiation of products of differentiable functions.
   a. Product rule0
   b. Thing
   c. Undefined
   d. Undefined

78. _____ is a method for differentiating expressions involving exponentiation the power operation.

Chapter 9. Exponential and Logarithmic Functions

    a. Thing
    c. Undefined
    b. Power rule0
    d. Undefined

79. In mathematics, science including computer science, linguistics and engineering, an _____ is, generally speaking, an independent variable or input to a function.
    a. Thing
    c. Undefined
    b. Argument0
    d. Undefined

80. A _____ is a deliberate process for transforming one or more inputs into one or more results.
    a. Calculation0
    c. Undefined
    b. Thing
    d. Undefined

81. In mathematics, factorization (British English: factorisation) or factoring is the decomposition of an object (for example, a number, a polynomial, or a matrix) into a product of other objects, or _____, which when multiplied together give the original.
    a. Thing
    c. Undefined
    b. Factors0
    d. Undefined

82. _____ is a mathematical operation, written a^n, involving two numbers, the base a and the exponent n.
    a. Exponentiating0
    c. Undefined
    b. Thing
    d. Undefined

83. _____ is a mathematical operation, written a^n, involving two numbers, the base a and the exponent n.
    a. Thing
    c. Undefined
    b. Exponentiation0
    d. Undefined

84. In mathematics, a _____ is the end result of a division problem. It can also be expressed as the number of times the divisor divides into the dividend.
    a. Quotient0
    c. Undefined
    b. Thing
    d. Undefined

85. The _____ is a method of finding the derivative of a function that is the quotient of two other functions for which derivatives exist.
    a. Quotient rule0
    c. Undefined
    b. Thing
    d. Undefined

86. A _____ is a numeral used to indicate a count. The most common use of the word today is to name the part of a fraction that tells the number or count of equal parts.
    a. Numerator0
    c. Undefined
    b. Thing
    d. Undefined

87. Mathematical _____ really refers to two distinct areas of research: the first is the application of the techniques of formal _____ to mathematics and mathematical reasoning, and the second, in the other direction, the application of mathematical techniques to the representation and analysis of formal _____.

Chapter 9. Exponential and Logarithmic Functions 137

    a. Logic0   b. Thing
    c. Undefined   d. Undefined

88. An _____ is a combination of numbers, operators, grouping symbols and/or free variables and bound variables arranged in a meaningful way which can be evaluated..
    a. Expression0   b. Thing
    c. Undefined   d. Undefined

89. Mathematical _____ is used to represent ideas.
    a. Notation0   b. Thing
    c. Undefined   d. Undefined

90. In mathematics, an _____ is a statement about the relative size or order of two objects.
    a. Inequality0   b. Thing
    c. Undefined   d. Undefined

91. A _____ is a negotiable instrument instructing a financial institution to pay a specific amount of a specific currency from a specific demand account held in the maker/depositor's name with that institution. Both the maker and payee may be natural persons or legal entities.
    a. Thing   b. Check0
    c. Undefined   d. Undefined

92. In mathematics, the _____ is the logarithm with base 10.
    a. Common logarithm0   b. Thing
    c. Undefined   d. Undefined

93. _____ is the symbol used to indicate the nth root of a number
    a. Thing   b. Radical0
    c. Undefined   d. Undefined

94. In mathematics, a _____ of a number x is a number r such that $r^2 = x$, or in words, a number r whose square (the result of multiplying the number by itself) is x.
    a. Square root0   b. Thing
    c. Undefined   d. Undefined

95. The word _____ is used in a variety of ways in mathematics.
    a. Thing   b. Index0
    c. Undefined   d. Undefined

96. _____ is a notation for writing numbers that is often used by scientists and mathematicians to make it easier to write large and small numbers.
    a. Scientific notation0   b. Thing
    c. Undefined   d. Undefined

97. _____, either of the curved-bracket punctuation marks that together make a set of _____

Chapter 9. Exponential and Logarithmic Functions

    a. Thing
    b. Parentheses0
    c. Undefined
    d. Undefined

98. In mathematics, _____ are any real number that is not a rational number ¡ª that is, it is a number which cannot be expressed as m/n, where m and n are integers.
    a. Irrational numbers0
    b. Thing
    c. Undefined
    d. Undefined

99. _____ is the process of reducing the number of significant digits in a number.
    a. Concept
    b. Rounding0
    c. Undefined
    d. Undefined

100. _____ are waste types containing radioactive chemical elements that do not have a practical purpose.
    a. Thing
    b. Radioactive waste0
    c. Undefined
    d. Undefined

101. A _____ is a landform that extends above the surrounding terrain in a limited area. A _____ is generally steeper than a hill, but there is no universally accepted standard definition for the height of a _____ or a hill although a _____ usually has an identifiable summit.
    a. Mountain0
    b. Thing
    c. Undefined
    d. Undefined

102. _____ is a way of expressing a number as a fraction of 100 per cent meaning "per hundred".
    a. Thing
    b. Percent0
    c. Undefined
    d. Undefined

103. An _____, also called a minor planet or planetoid, comes from a class of atsronomical objects.
    a. Asteroid0
    b. Thing
    c. Undefined
    d. Undefined

104. _____ is the scientific study of celestial objects such as stars, planets, comets, and galaxies; and phenomena that originate outside the Earth's atmosphere.
    a. Thing
    b. Astronomy0
    c. Undefined
    d. Undefined

105. A _____, as defined by the International Astronomical Union , is a celestial body orbiting a star or stellar remnant that is massive enough to be rounded by its own gravity, not massive enough to cause thermonuclear fusion in its core, and has cleared its neighboring region of planetesimals.
    a. Thing
    b. Planet0
    c. Undefined
    d. Undefined

106. In geometry, a _____ (Greek words diairo = divide and metro = measure) of a circle is any straight line segment that passes through the centre and whose endpoints are on the circular boundary, or, in more modern usage, the length of such a line segment. When using the word in the more modern sense, one speaks of the _____ rather than a _____, because all diameters of a circle have the same length. This length is twice the radius. The _____ of a circle is also the longest chord that the circle has.

Chapter 9. Exponential and Logarithmic Functions

a. Thing
c. Undefined
b. Diameter0
d. Undefined

107. In linear algebra, a _____ of a matrix A is the determinant of some smaller square matrix, cut down from A.
a. Minor0
c. Undefined
b. Thing
d. Undefined

108. In mathematics, an _____, mean, or central tendency of a data set refers to a measure of the "middle" or "expected" value of the data set.
a. Average0
c. Undefined
b. Concept
d. Undefined

109. The _____ is the process of converting elements in one basis to another when both describe the same elements of the finite field $GF(p^m)$.
a. Thing
c. Undefined
b. Change of base0
d. Undefined

110. The _____ is the process of converting elements in one basis to another when both describe the same elements of the finite field $GF(p^m)$.
a. Thing
c. Undefined
b. Change of bases0
d. Undefined

111. _____ is the transport of people on a trip/journey or the process or time involved in a person or object moving from one location to another.
a. Travel0
c. Undefined
b. Thing
d. Undefined

112. In mathematics, the additive inverse, or _____ of a number n is the number that, when added to n, yields zero. The additive inverse of n is denoted −n. For example, 7 is −7, because 7 + (−7) = 0, and the additive inverse of −0.3 is 0.3, because −0.3 + 0.3 = 0.
a. Opposite0
c. Undefined
b. Thing
d. Undefined

113. In mathematics, the _____ of a number n is the number that, when added to n, yields zero. The _____ of n is denoted −n. For example, 7 is −7, because 7 + (−7) = 0, and the _____ of −0.3 is 0.3, because −0.3 + 0.3 = 0.
a. Additive inverse0
c. Undefined
b. Thing
d. Undefined

114. In elementary algebra, an _____ is a set that contains every real number between two indicated numbers and may contain the two numbers themselves.
a. Thing
c. Undefined
b. Interval0
d. Undefined

115. _____ is the notation in which permitted values for a variable are expressed as ranging over a certain interval; "5 < x < 9" is an example of the application of _____.

Chapter 9. Exponential and Logarithmic Functions

    a. Interval notation0   b. Thing
    c. Undefined   d. Undefined

116. _____ variables are variables other than the independent variable that may bear any effect on the behavior of the subject being studied.
    a. Extraneous0   b. Thing
    c. Undefined   d. Undefined

117. A _____ is a number that is less than zero.
    a. Negative number0   b. Thing
    c. Undefined   d. Undefined

118. _____ forms part of thinking. Considered the most complex of all intellectual functions, _____ has been defined as higher-order cognitive process that requires the modulation and control of more routine or fundamental skills.
    a. Problem solving0   b. Thing
    c. Undefined   d. Undefined

119. A _____ are accounts maintained by commercial banks, savings and loan associations, credit unions, and mutual savings banks that pay interest but can not be used directly as money by, for example, writing a cheque.
    a. Thing   b. Savings account0
    c. Undefined   d. Undefined

120. _____ is a term used in accounting, economics and finance with reference to the fact that assets with finite lives lose value over time.
    a. Thing   b. Depreciation0
    c. Undefined   d. Undefined

121. The _____ relative to a specified or implied reference level.
    a. Decibel0   b. Thing
    c. Undefined   d. Undefined

122. A _____ is a set of possible values that a variable can take on in order to satisfy a given set of conditions, which may include equations and inequalities.
    a. Thing   b. Solution set0
    c. Undefined   d. Undefined

123. In geometry, a _____ is a special kind of point, usually a corner of a polygon, polyhedron, or higher dimensional polytope. In the geometry of curves a _____ is a point of where the first derivative of curvature is zero. In graph theory, a _____ is the fundamental unit out of which graphs are formed
    a. Thing   b. Vertex0
    c. Undefined   d. Undefined

124. In mathematics, the _____ is a conic section generated by the intersection of a right circular conical surface and a plane parallel to a generating straight line of that surface. It can also be defined as locus of points in a plane which are equidistant from a given point.

Chapter 9. Exponential and Logarithmic Functions

a. Thing
b. Parabola0
c. Undefined
d. Undefined

125. _____ is the logarithm to the base e, where e is an irrational constant approximately equal to 2.718281828459.
a. Thing
b. Natural logarithm0
c. Undefined
d. Undefined

126. In geometry, the _____ of an object is a point in some sense in the middle of the object.
a. Thing
b. Center0
c. Undefined
d. Undefined

127. In Euclidean geometry, an _____ is a closed segment of a differentiable curve in the two-dimensional plane; for example, a circular _____ is a segment of a circle.
a. Concept
b. Arc0
c. Undefined
d. Undefined

128. Initial objects are also called _____, and terminal objects are also called final.
a. Thing
b. Coterminal0
c. Undefined
d. Undefined

129. In banking and accountancy, the outstanding _____ is the amount of money owned, or due, that remains in a deposit account or a loan account at a given date, after all past remittances, payments and withdrawal have been accounted for.
a. Balance0
b. Thing
c. Undefined
d. Undefined

130. The act of _____ is the calculated approximation of a result which is usable even if input data may be incomplete, uncertain, or noisy.
a. Thing
b. Estimating0
c. Undefined
d. Undefined

131. In descriptive statistics, using the _____ is a way of providing estimation of proportions of the data that should fall above and below a given value.
a. Percentile0
b. Thing
c. Undefined
d. Undefined

132. In probability theory and statistics, a _____ is a number dividing the higher half of a sample, a population, or a probability distribution from the lower half.
a. Median0
b. Concept
c. Undefined
d. Undefined

133. An _____ or member of a set is an object that when collected together make up the set.
a. Element0
b. Thing
c. Undefined
d. Undefined

Chapter 9. Exponential and Logarithmic Functions

134. _____ is a set, with some particular properties and usually some additional structure, such as the operations of addition or multiplication, for instance.
- a. Thing
- b. Space0
- c. Undefined
- d. Undefined

135. _____ of an object is its speed in a particular direction.
- a. Velocity0
- b. Thing
- c. Undefined
- d. Undefined

136. A _____ is a polynomial consisting of three terms; in other words, it is the sum of three monomials.
- a. Trinomial0
- b. Thing
- c. Undefined
- d. Undefined

137. The term _____ can refer to an integer which is the square of some other integer, or an algebraic expression that can be factored as the square of some other expression.
- a. Perfect square0
- b. Thing
- c. Undefined
- d. Undefined

138. In mathematics, a _____, formed by the composition of one function on another, represents the application of the former to the result of the application of the latter to the argument of the composite.
- a. Function composition0
- b. Thing
- c. Undefined
- d. Undefined

139. U.S. liquid _____ is legally defined as 231 cubic inches, and is equal to 3.785411784 litres or abotu 0.13368 cubic feet. This is the most common definition of a _____. The U.S. fluid ounce is defined as 1/128 of a U.S. _____.
- a. Thing
- b. Gallon0
- c. Undefined
- d. Undefined

140. _____ is a synonym for information.
- a. Thing
- b. Data0
- c. Undefined
- d. Undefined

141. The _____ of a geographic location is its height above a fixed reference point, often the mean sea level.
- a. Elevation0
- b. Thing
- c. Undefined
- d. Undefined

142. A _____ is a movement of an object in a circular motion. A two-dimensional object rotates around a center (or point) of _____. A three-dimensional object rotates around a line called an axis. If the axis of _____ is within the body, the body is said to rotate upon itself, or spinâ€"which implies relative speed and perhaps free-movement with angular momentum. A circular motion about an external point, e.g. the Earth about the Sun, is called an orbit or more properly an orbital revolution.
- a. Thing
- b. Rotation0
- c. Undefined
- d. Undefined

Chapter 9. Exponential and Logarithmic Functions

143. _____ is often used to describe the measurement of the steepness, incline, gradient, or grade of a straight line. The _____ is defined as the ratio of the "rise" divided by the "run" between two points on a line, or in other words, the ratio of the altitude change to the horizontal distance between any two points on the line.
    a. Slope0
    b. Thing
    c. Undefined
    d. Undefined

144. In mathematics, an _____ .
    a. Thing
    b. Ellipse0
    c. Undefined
    d. Undefined

Chapter 10. Conic Sections

1. _____ is the study of quantity, structure, space, and change. Historically, _____ developed from counting, calculation, measurement, and the study of the shapes and motions of physical objects, through the use of abstraction and deductive reasoning.
   a. Mathematics10
   b. -equivalence
   c. Undefined
   d. Undefined

2. By _____ we mean the cumulative frequency, counting in from the nearer end.
   a. Depth10
   b. -equivalence
   c. Undefined
   d. Undefined

3. A <U>point </U>is an undefined term. We usually represent this by a dot, but a _____ actually has no dimension. A capital letter names any _____.
   a. -equivalence
   b. Point10
   c. Undefined
   d. Undefined

4. A <U>circle</U> is a series of points the same distance from a given point, called the center.
   a. -equivalence
   b. Circle10
   c. Undefined
   d. Undefined

5. An <U>equation</U> is represented by two expressions that have the same value.
   a. ADE classification
   b. Equation10
   c. Undefined
   d. Undefined

6. A _____ is a multiplicative factor of a certain object such as a variable (for example, the coefficients of a polynomial), a basis vector, a basis function and so on. Usually, the objects and the coefficients are indexed in the same way, leading to expressions such as a1x1 + a2x2 + a3x3 + ... where an is the _____ of the variable xn for each n = 1, 2, 3, ...
   a. -equivalence
   b. Coefficient10
   c. Undefined
   d. Undefined

7. A number that does not change in value in a given situation is a _____.
   a. Constant10
   b. -equivalence
   c. Undefined
   d. Undefined

8. _____ is used synonymously for variable.
   a. Factor10
   b. -equivalence
   c. Undefined
   d. Undefined

9. When a value makes an equation true, it is called a <U>solution</U>. 3 is a _____ of x + 2 = 5,
   a. Solution10
   b. -equivalence
   c. Undefined
   d. Undefined

10. A quadrilateral with 4 equal sides and all right angles is called a <U>square.</U>
    a. Square10
    b. -equivalence
    c. Undefined
    d. Undefined

11. Whenever a number is raised to the second power, we can also say that the number is _____.

Chapter 10. Conic Sections

a. -equivalence
c. Undefined
b. Squared10
d. Undefined

12. A _____ is a number or variable, or the product or quotient of a number or variable.
a. -equivalence
c. Undefined
b. Term10
d. Undefined

13. The very fact that we are measuring objects with respect to some characteristic implies that the objects differ in that characteristic; or stated in another way, that the characteristic can take on a number of different values. These properties or characteristics of an object that can assume two or more different values are referred to as a _____.
a. Variable10
c. Undefined
b. -equivalence
d. Undefined

14. The word _____ can have three meanings: In _____ theory, a _____ is an abstract object consisting of vertices (or nodes) and edges (or arcs) between pairs of vertices. The _____ of a function f : X ¨ Y is the set of all pairs (x,f(x)) The _____ of a relation, a generalisation of the _____ of a function.
a. Graph10
c. Undefined
b. -equivalence
d. Undefined

15. If one number is to the right of another number on the number line, this number is <U>greater than </U>the number on the left. The symbol that is used is >.
a. -equivalence
c. Undefined
b. Greater than10
d. Undefined

16. The _____ is t the point where a graph intersects the y-axis and is found by setting x = 0 and then sovling for the y-value.
a. Y-intercept10
c. Undefined
b. -equivalence
d. Undefined

17. A _____ is an undefined term. However, it is often thought of as a series of points. A _____ has one dimension - length. A _____ is either named by a lower case letter or by two points on the _____.
a. -equivalence
c. Undefined
b. Line10
d. Undefined

18. When a given number is the product of another number by itself, the another number is called the <U>square root</U>. Ex: 25 = 5 x 5 so 5 is the _____ of 25.
a. Square root10
c. Undefined
b. -equivalence
d. Undefined

19. Addition (or summation) is one of the basic operations of arithmetic. In its simplest form, addition combines two numbers, the augend and addend, into a single number, the _____. Adding more numbers can be viewed as repeated addition. (Repeated addition of the number one is the most basic form of counting.) By extension, the addition of zero numbers, one number, or infinitely many numbers can be defined.
a. Sum10
c. Undefined
b. -equivalence
d. Undefined

Chapter 10. Conic Sections

20. A <U>line segment </U>is a piece of a line. The _____ has definite length and is named by the two endpoints.
   a. Line segment10
   b. -equivalence
   c. Undefined
   d. Undefined

21. The _____ is often confused with the median. The Median is a statistic for the distribution whereas the _____ provides a statistic for an interval; it is the center of the interval; the arithmetic average of the upper and lower limits.
   a. -equivalence
   b. Midpoint10
   c. Undefined
   d. Undefined

22. The <U>center of a circle </U>is the given point all the points of the circle come from.
   a. -equivalence
   b. Center of a circle10
   c. Undefined
   d. Undefined

23. The point of intersection of the horizontal and vertical axes in the rectangular coordinate plane is the _____. It is is expressed as the ordered pair (0,0).
   a. Origin10
   b. ADE classification
   c. Undefined
   d. Undefined

24. A _____ is a concrete example of an item or a specification against which all others may be measured. For example, there are "primary standards" for length, mass (see Kilogram standard), and other units of measure, kept by laboratories and standards organizations.
   a. -equivalence
   b. Standard10
   c. Undefined
   d. Undefined

25. The <U>radius</U> of a circle is the distance from the center to the circle.
   a. Radius10
   b. -equivalence
   c. Undefined
   d. Undefined

26. <U>A <U>vertical line </U>goes up and down or from North to South.</U>
   a. -equivalence
   b. Vertical line10
   c. Undefined
   d. Undefined

27. A <U>plane</U> is an undefined term. We can think of it as a series of lines having 2 dimensions, width and length.
   a. -equivalence
   b. Plane10
   c. Undefined
   d. Undefined

28. Any polygon that has 3 sides is called a <U>triangle</U>.
   a. Triangle10
   b. -equivalence
   c. Undefined
   d. Undefined

29. A number that is raised to a power, or _____ of an exponential function. This finds common use, for example, in the depiction of numbers, for instance, 10 is the _____ used in the decimal system, whereas 2 is the _____ in the binary numeral system.

Chapter 10. Conic Sections

    a. Base10
    b. -equivalence
    c. Undefined
    d. Undefined

30. _____ are characteristics or properties of an object that can take on one or more different values.
    a. -equivalence
    b. Variables10
    c. Undefined
    d. Undefined

31. A _____ is simply a polynomial with two terms such as this example: 2x + 7.
    a. Binomial10
    b. -equivalence
    c. Undefined
    d. Undefined

32. An <U>axis</U> is one of the number lines found on the rectangular coordinate system. The x asis is the horizontal number line while the y _____ is the vertical number line.
    a. ADE classification
    b. Axis10
    c. Undefined
    d. Undefined

33. The bottom part of any fraction represents the number of pieces in one whole unit. This bottom part is called the <U>denominator.</U>
    a. -equivalence
    b. Denominator10
    c. Undefined
    d. Undefined

34. _____ is the change in x between two points
    a. -equivalence
    b. Run10
    c. Undefined
    d. Undefined

35. The highest number in a list of values is called the <U>maximum.</U>
    a. Maximum10
    b. -equivalence
    c. Undefined
    d. Undefined

36. The lowest number in a list of values is called the <U>minimum</U>.
    a. -equivalence
    b. Minimum10
    c. Undefined
    d. Undefined

37. The answer to subtraction is called the <U>difference</U>.
    a. Difference10
    b. -equivalence
    c. Undefined
    d. Undefined

38. A _____ is a well-defined collection of objects considered as a whole.
    a. Set10
    b. -equivalence
    c. Undefined
    d. Undefined

39. A quadrilateral with opposite sides equal and parallel and containing all right angles is called a <U>rectangle.</U>
    a. Rectangle10
    b. -equivalence
    c. Undefined
    d. Undefined

Chapter 10. Conic Sections

40. The <U>opposite</U> of a number is the number that makes a sum zero. In most cases, this means just to change the sign. 3 is the _____ of -3.
    a. ADE classification
    b. Opposite10
    c. Undefined
    d. Undefined

41. A measure of variability, the _____ is the distance from the lowest to the highest score.
    a. Range10
    b. -equivalence
    c. Undefined
    d. Undefined

42. _____ (or summation) is one of the basic operations of arithmetic. In its simplest form, _____ combines two numbers, the augend and addend, into a single number, the sum.
    a. ADE classification
    b. Addition10
    c. Undefined
    d. Undefined

43. <U>Perimeter</U> is the distance around a polygon. It can be found by adding the lengths of all sides.
    a. -equivalence
    b. Perimeter10
    c. Undefined
    d. Undefined

44. A <U>hypotenuse</U> occurs in a right triangle and is the side opposite the right angle. It will also be the longest side of a right triangle.
    a. Hypotenuse10
    b. -equivalence
    c. Undefined
    d. Undefined

45. A <U>quadratic</U> contains at least one squared term.
    a. -equivalence
    b. Quadratic10
    c. Undefined
    d. Undefined

Chapter 11. Sequences, Series, and the Binomial Theorem

1. Addition (or summation) is one of the basic operations of arithmetic. In its simplest form, addition combines two numbers, the augend and addend, into a single number, the _____. Adding more numbers can be viewed as repeated addition. (Repeated addition of the number one is the most basic form of counting.) By extension, the addition of zero numbers, one number, or infinitely many numbers can be defined.
   - a. -equivalence
   - b. Sum11
   - c. Undefined
   - d. Undefined

2. An irrational number is any real number that is not a rational number, i.e., one that cannot be written as a ratio of two integers, i.e., it is not of the form a/b where a and b are integers and b is not zero. It can readily be shown that the _____ are precisely those numbers whose expansion in any given base (decimal, binary, etc) never ends and never enters a periodic pattern, but no mathematician takes that to be a definition. Almost all real numbers are irrational, in a sense which is defined more precisely below. Some _____ are algebraic numbers, such as ā2, the square root of two, and 3 ā5, the cube root of 5; others are transcendental numbers such as fî and e.
   - a. Irrational numbers11
   - b. ADE classification
   - c. Undefined
   - d. Undefined

3. _____ is the study of quantity, structure, space, and change. Historically, _____ developed from counting, calculation, measurement, and the study of the shapes and motions of physical objects, through the use of abstraction and deductive reasoning.
   - a. Mathematics11
   - b. -equivalence
   - c. Undefined
   - d. Undefined

4. If one number is to the right of another number on the number line, this number is <U>greater than </U>the number on the left. The symbol that is used is >.
   - a. Greater than11
   - b. -equivalence
   - c. Undefined
   - d. Undefined

5. A _____ is a well-defined collection of objects considered as a whole.
   - a. Set11
   - b. -equivalence
   - c. Undefined
   - d. Undefined

6. A _____ is a number or variable, or the product or quotient of a number or variable.
   - a. Term11
   - b. -equivalence
   - c. Undefined
   - d. Undefined

7. A measure of variability, the _____ is the distance from the lowest to the highest score.
   - a. Range11
   - b. -equivalence
   - c. Undefined
   - d. Undefined

8. The Greek letter _____ indicates summation.
   - a. Sigma11
   - b. -equivalence
   - c. Undefined
   - d. Undefined

9. When a value makes an equation true, it is called a <U>solution</U>. 3 is a _____ of x + 2 = 5,
   - a. Solution11
   - b. -equivalence
   - c. Undefined
   - d. Undefined

10. The _____ in a disttribution or in an interval is the least value.
   a. -equivalence
   b. Lower limit11
   c. Undefined
   d. Undefined

11. In a distribution of data or in an interval of data, the _____ is the greatest value.
   a. ADE classification
   b. Upper limit11
   c. Undefined
   d. Undefined

12. By _____ we mean collecting observations made upon our environment -- observations, which are the results of measurements using clocks, balances, measuring rods, counting operations, or other objectively defined measuring instruments or procedures. _____ may mean simply counting the number of times a particular property occurs.
   a. -equivalence
   b. Data11
   c. Undefined
   d. Undefined

13. _____ or arithmetics (from the Greek word áñéèìùò = number) in common usage is a branch of (or the forerunner of) mathematics which records elementary properties of certain operations on numerals, though in usage by professional mathematicians, it often is treated as a synonym for number theory.
   a. Arithmetic11
   b. ADE classification
   c. Undefined
   d. Undefined

14. The most important measure of central tendency, and one of the basic building blocks of all statistical analysis, is the arithmetic <U>mean.</U> It is simply the sum of all the set of values divided by the number of values involved. It can also be called the average.
   a. -equivalence
   b. Mean11
   c. Undefined
   d. Undefined

15. _____ is used synonymously for variable.
   a. -equivalence
   b. Factor11
   c. Undefined
   d. Undefined

16. The answer to subtraction is called the <U>difference</U>.
   a. -equivalence
   b. Difference11
   c. Undefined
   d. Undefined

17. A number that does not change in value in a given situation is a _____.
   a. -equivalence
   b. Constant11
   c. Undefined
   d. Undefined

18. Any time one number is on the left side of another number on a number line, the first number is <U>less than </U>the second number. The symbol for this is <.
   a. -equivalence
   b. Less than11
   c. Undefined
   d. Undefined

19. A closed shape whose sides are all line segments is called a <U>polygon.</U>

Chapter 11. Sequences, Series, and the Binomial Theorem

a. Polygon11
c. Undefined
b. -equivalence
d. Undefined

20. _____ is a central branch of mathematics, developed from algebra and geometry, and built on two major complementary ideas, differential _____ and integral _____.
a. Calculus11
c. Undefined
b. -equivalence
d. Undefined

21. When a given number is multiplied by any or all natural numbers, <U>multiples</U> are formed.2, 4, 6 are all examples of multiples of 2.
a. -equivalence
c. Undefined
b. Multiple11
d. Undefined

22. A _____ is the relationship between two quantities. It is expressed as the quotient of two numbers, or as two numbers separated by a colon (pronounced "to"). A number that can be written as a _____ of two integers is a rational number.
a. Ratio11
c. Undefined
b. -equivalence
d. Undefined

23. _____ (or summation) is one of the basic operations of arithmetic. In its simplest form, _____ combines two numbers, the augend and addend, into a single number, the sum.
a. ADE classification
c. Undefined
b. Addition11
d. Undefined

24. A <U>point </U>is an undefined term. We usually represent this by a dot, but a _____ actually has no dimension. A capital letter names any _____.
a. -equivalence
c. Undefined
b. Point11
d. Undefined

25. The <U>exponent </U>indicates how many of the base to multiply together to get the product. When 5 to the third power is 125, then 3 is the _____ and can also be called a power.
a. Exponent11
c. Undefined
b. ADE classification
d. Undefined

26. A _____, also referred to as a universe, is any well-defined collection of things. By well-defined we mean that the members of the _____ are spelled out, or an unequivocal statement is made as to which things belong in it and which do not.
a. Population11
c. Undefined
b. -equivalence
d. Undefined

27. By _____ we mean the cumulative frequency, counting in from the nearer end.
a. -equivalence
c. Undefined
b. Depth11
d. Undefined

Chapter 11. Sequences, Series, and the Binomial Theorem

28. An _____ is an indication of the value of an unknown quantity based on observed data. More formally, an _____ is the particular value of an estimator that is obtained from a particular sample of data and used to indicate the value of a parameter.
    a. ADE classification
    b. Estimate11
    c. Undefined
    d. Undefined

29. _____ is an estimate of the decrease in the value of an asset, caused by "wear and tear", obsolescence, or impairment. The use of _____ affects a company's (or an individual's) financial statements, and, in some countries, their taxes.
    a. Depreciation11
    b. -equivalence
    c. Undefined
    d. Undefined

30. The word _____ can have three meanings: In _____ theory, a _____ is an abstract object consisting of vertices (or nodes) and edges (or arcs) between pairs of vertices. The _____ of a function f : X ¨ Y is the set of all pairs (x,f(x)) The _____ of a relation, a generalisation of the _____ of a function.
    a. Graph11
    b. -equivalence
    c. Undefined
    d. Undefined

31. A _____ is simply a polynomial with two terms such as this example: 2x + 7.
    a. Binomial11
    b. -equivalence
    c. Undefined
    d. Undefined

32. A _____ provides a quantitative description of the likely occurrence of a particular event. _____ is conventionally expressed on a scale from 0 to 1; a rare event has a _____ close to 0, a very common event has a _____ close to 1. _____ is calculated as the ratio of the number of favorable events to the total number of possible events.
    a. -equivalence
    b. Probability11
    c. Undefined
    d. Undefined

33. Any polygon that has 3 sides is called a <U>triangle</U>.
    a. Triangle11
    b. -equivalence
    c. Undefined
    d. Undefined

34. A _____ is a multiplicative factor of a certain object such as a variable (for example, the coefficients of a polynomial), a basis vector, a basis function and so on. Usually, the objects and the coefficients are indexed in the same way, leading to expressions such as a1x1 + a2x2 + a3x3 + ... where an is the _____ of the variable xn for each n = 1, 2, 3, ...
    a. -equivalence
    b. Coefficient11
    c. Undefined
    d. Undefined

35. The very fact that we are measuring objects with respect to some characteristic implies that the objects differ in that characteristic; or stated in another way, that the characteristic can take on a number of different values. These properties or characteristics of an object that can assume two or more different values are referred to as a _____.
    a. Variable11
    b. -equivalence
    c. Undefined
    d. Undefined

36. An _____ combines numbers, operators, and/or variables but contains no equal or inequality sign.
   a. ADE classification
   b. Expression11
   c. Undefined
   d. Undefined

37. <U>Perimeter</U> is the distance around a polygon. It can be found by adding the lengths of all sides.
   a. Perimeter11
   b. -equivalence
   c. Undefined
   d. Undefined

38. A quadrilateral with opposite sides equal and parallel and containing all right angles is called a <U>rectangle.</U>
   a. Rectangle11
   b. -equivalence
   c. Undefined
   d. Undefined

39. A quadrilateral with 4 equal sides and all right angles is called a <U>square.</U>
   a. Square11
   b. -equivalence
   c. Undefined
   d. Undefined

40. A <U>quadratic</U> contains at least one squared term.
   a. -equivalence
   b. Quadratic11
   c. Undefined
   d. Undefined

41. <U>Twice</U> means to multiply by 2.
   a. Twice11
   b. -equivalence
   c. Undefined
   d. Undefined

Chapter 1

1. a	2. a	3. b	4. b	5. a	6. b	7. b	8. b	9. a	10. b
11. b	12. a	13. b	14. b	15. b	16. b	17. b	18. a	19. b	20. a
21. b	22. a	23. b	24. b	25. a	26. a	27. a	28. b	29. a	30. a
31. b	32. b	33. b	34. a	35. b	36. a	37. a	38. a	39. b	40. b
41. b	42. b	43. a	44. b	45. a	46. b	47. a	48. b	49. a	50. a
51. b	52. b	53. a	54. b	55. b	56. b	57. b	58. b	59. a	60. a
61. a	62. b	63. b	64. a	65. a	66. b	67. b	68. a	69. b	70. a
71. a	72. b	73. a	74. b	75. a	76. b	77. a	78. a	79. a	80. a
81. a	82. a	83. a	84. b	85. a	86. a	87. a	88. b	89. a	90. a
91. b	92. a	93. a	94. a	95. a	96. a	97. b	98. a	99. a	100. a
101. b	102. a	103. a	104. a	105. b	106. b	107. a	108. a	109. b	110. a
111. a	112. b	113. b	114. a	115. a	116. a	117. a	118. a	119. b	120. a
121. a	122. a	123. a	124. b	125. a	126. a	127. b	128. a	129. b	130. b
131. b	132. a	133. a	134. a	135. a	136. a	137. b	138. b	139. a	140. b
141. a	142. a								

Chapter 2

1. b	2. a	3. b	4. b	5. b	6. a	7. a	8. b	9. a	10. b
11. a	12. b	13. a	14. a	15. b	16. a	17. a	18. a	19. a	20. b
21. b	22. b	23. a	24. b	25. b	26. b	27. a	28. b	29. b	30. a
31. a	32. b	33. a	34. b	35. a	36. b	37. b	38. b	39. b	40. a
41. a	42. a	43. a	44. a	45. b	46. b	47. b	48. a	49. b	50. a
51. b	52. a	53. a	54. a	55. b	56. b	57. a	58. a	59. a	60. a
61. b	62. a	63. b	64. b	65. b	66. b	67. b	68. b	69. a	70. a
71. b	72. a	73. b	74. a	75. b	76. b	77. b	78. a	79. a	80. b
81. b	82. b	83. a	84. a	85. a	86. a	87. b	88. b	89. a	90. a
91. b	92. a	93. b	94. a	95. b	96. b	97. b	98. b	99. b	100. b
101. a	102. a	103. a	104. a	105. a	106. a	107. b	108. b	109. b	110. b
111. a	112. a	113. a	114. a	115. b	116. b	117. b	118. b	119. a	120. a
121. b	122. b	123. b	124. a	125. b	126. a	127. a	128. b	129. b	130. b
131. b	132. a	133. b	134. a	135. b	136. b	137. a	138. b	139. a	140. a
141. b	142. b	143. b	144. b	145. b	146. a	147. b	148. b	149. a	150. b
151. a	152. a	153. b	154. a	155. b	156. b	157. b	158. a	159. a	160. a
161. a	162. a	163. b	164. b	165. a	166. a	167. a			

ANSWER KEY

Chapter 3

1. b	2. b	3. a	4. a	5. a	6. a	7. a	8. a	9. b	10. a
11. b	12. b	13. a	14. b	15. a	16. a	17. b	18. a	19. a	20. b
21. b	22. b	23. b	24. a	25. a	26. a	27. a	28. b	29. b	30. a
31. a	32. b	33. b	34. a	35. b	36. a	37. a	38. b	39. b	40. b
41. a	42. a	43. a	44. b	45. b	46. b	47. a	48. a	49. a	50. a
51. a	52. a	53. a	54. b	55. b	56. b	57. a	58. b	59. b	60. a
61. b	62. a	63. b	64. a	65. a	66. b	67. a	68. b	69. b	70. a
71. b	72. b	73. a	74. b	75. a	76. a	77. a	78. b	79. b	80. b
81. b	82. b	83. a	84. b	85. a	86. b	87. a	88. b	89. b	90. a
91. b	92. a	93. a	94. a	95. a	96. b	97. a	98. b	99. b	100. a
101. a	102. a	103. a	104. b	105. b	106. a	107. b	108. b	109. b	110. b
111. b	112. a	113. b	114. a	115. b	116. a	117. b	118. b	119. a	120. a
121. a	122. a	123. a	124. a	125. a	126. a	127. b	128. a	129. a	130. b
131. b	132. b	133. b	134. a	135. b	136. b	137. b	138. a	139. b	140. b
141. b	142. a	143. b	144. b	145. a	146. a	147. a	148. a	149. b	150. a
151. a	152. b	153. b	154. b	155. b	156. a	157. b	158. a	159. b	160. a

Chapter 4

1. b	2. b	3. b	4. a	5. b	6. a	7. b	8. a	9. b	10. a
11. a	12. a	13. a	14. b	15. b	16. b	17. a	18. a	19. a	20. a
21. a	22. b	23. a	24. b	25. b	26. a	27. a	28. b	29. b	30. b
31. a	32. b	33. a	34. b	35. a	36. a	37. b	38. b	39. a	40. a
41. b	42. a	43. b	44. b	45. b	46. b	47. a	48. b	49. a	50. a
51. b	52. b	53. b	54. b	55. a	56. b	57. a	58. b	59. a	60. a
61. b	62. a	63. a	64. b	65. a	66. a	67. a	68. b	69. a	70. b
71. b	72. b	73. a	74. b	75. a	76. b	77. b	78. a	79. b	80. a
81. b	82. a	83. b	84. a	85. a	86. b	87. a	88. a	89. b	90. b
91. a	92. a	93. a	94. b	95. b	96. a	97. a	98. b	99. b	100. a
101. b	102. b	103. a	104. b	105. a	106. a	107. a	108. b	109. a	110. a
111. b	112. b	113. b	114. b	115. b	116. a	117. a	118. a	119. a	120. b
121. a	122. b	123. b	124. a	125. a	126. b	127. a	128. a		

Chapter 5

1. a	2. a	3. a	4. a	5. a	6. b	7. b	8. b	9. b	10. b
11. a	12. b	13. a	14. b	15. a	16. b	17. b	18. a	19. a	20. a
21. b	22. b	23. a	24. b	25. b	26. b	27. b	28. b	29. b	30. a
31. a	32. b	33. a	34. a	35. a	36. a	37. a	38. b	39. b	40. a
41. a	42. b	43. a	44. a	45. b	46. b	47. b	48. b	49. a	50. a
51. b	52. a	53. b	54. a	55. a	56. a	57. a	58. a	59. b	60. a
61. b	62. b	63. b	64. a	65. b	66. a	67. b	68. a	69. a	70. a
71. b	72. b	73. b	74. a	75. a	76. b	77. b	78. a	79. b	80. b
81. a	82. a	83. b	84. a	85. a	86. b	87. a	88. b	89. a	90. b
91. b	92. a	93. b	94. b	95. a	96. a	97. b	98. b	99. b	100. b
101. b	102. a	103. a	104. b	105. a	106. b	107. b	108. b	109. a	110. a
111. a	112. a	113. b	114. a	115. b	116. b	117. b	118. a	119. a	120. a
121. b	122. b	123. a	124. b	125. b	126. b	127. b	128. a	129. a	130. a
131. a	132. b	133. b	134. a	135. a	136. b	137. b	138. a		

Chapter 6

1. a	2. a	3. a	4. a	5. a	6. b	7. a	8. a	9. a	10. a
11. b	12. b	13. b	14. b	15. a	16. b	17. a	18. a	19. b	20. a
21. b	22. b	23. b	24. b	25. a	26. b	27. a	28. a	29. b	30. b
31. a	32. a	33. a	34. b	35. a	36. b	37. b	38. b	39. b	40. a
41. a	42. b	43. a	44. b	45. b	46. a	47. a	48. b	49. a	50. b
51. a	52. b	53. a	54. b	55. b	56. a	57. b	58. b	59. b	60. b
61. b	62. a	63. a	64. b	65. b	66. a	67. b	68. a	69. a	70. b
71. a	72. a	73. a	74. b	75. a	76. a	77. a	78. b	79. a	80. b
81. a	82. a	83. b	84. a	85. a	86. b	87. b	88. a	89. a	90. b
91. a	92. a	93. b	94. b	95. b	96. a	97. a	98. a	99. b	100. a
101. b	102. a	103. a	104. a	105. b	106. a	107. a	108. a	109. b	110. a
111. b	112. a	113. a	114. a	115. b	116. b	117. a	118. a	119. a	120. b
121. b	122. a	123. a	124. b	125. b	126. b	127. a	128. a	129. a	130. a
131. a	132. a	133. a	134. a	135. a	136. a	137. a	138. a	139. a	140. b
141. b	142. a	143. a	144. a	145. a	146. b	147. b	148. a	149. b	150. b

ANSWER KEY

Chapter 7

1. a	2. a	3. a	4. a	5. b	6. a	7. b	8. b	9. b	10. a
11. a	12. a	13. b	14. b	15. b	16. a	17. b	18. b	19. a	20. b
21. b	22. b	23. b	24. a	25. b	26. b	27. b	28. a	29. a	30. a
31. b	32. a	33. b	34. a	35. b	36. b	37. a	38. a	39. a	40. b
41. b	42. a	43. b	44. a	45. b	46. b	47. b	48. a	49. b	50. b
51. a	52. a	53. b	54. a	55. b	56. b	57. b	58. a	59. b	60. a
61. a	62. b	63. b	64. a	65. b	66. b	67. a	68. b	69. a	70. a
71. a	72. a	73. a	74. b	75. b	76. a	77. a	78. a	79. a	80. a
81. b	82. b	83. b	84. a	85. b	86. a	87. b	88. a	89. b	90. a
91. a	92. b	93. a	94. a	95. a	96. a	97. b	98. a	99. a	100. b
101. b	102. a	103. a	104. a	105. b	106. a	107. b	108. b	109. b	110. b
111. a	112. b	113. a	114. b	115. a	116. b	117. a	118. b	119. b	120. b
121. b	122. a	123. b	124. a	125. b	126. a	127. b	128. a	129. b	130. a
131. a	132. a	133. a	134. b	135. b	136. a	137. b	138. a	139. b	140. a
141. b	142. b	143. b	144. b	145. b	146. a	147. b	148. b		

Chapter 8

1. a	2. b	3. b	4. a	5. a	6. a	7. a	8. a	9. a	10. a
11. b	12. b	13. b	14. a	15. b	16. a	17. a	18. b	19. b	20. a
21. a	22. a	23. b	24. a	25. b	26. b	27. b	28. b	29. a	30. b
31. b	32. a	33. a	34. a	35. b	36. a	37. b	38. a	39. b	40. b
41. b	42. b	43. a	44. a	45. b	46. a	47. b	48. b	49. a	50. a
51. a	52. a	53. b	54. b	55. b	56. a	57. b	58. a	59. a	60. a
61. b	62. b	63. b	64. a	65. b	66. b	67. b	68. a	69. a	70. b
71. a	72. a	73. b	74. a	75. a	76. a	77. a	78. a	79. a	80. b
81. a	82. a	83. a	84. a	85. a	86. b	87. b	88. b	89. a	90. b
91. b	92. b	93. a	94. b	95. b	96. a	97. a	98. a	99. b	100. b
101. a	102. a	103. b	104. a	105. a	106. a	107. a	108. b	109. b	110. b
111. b	112. a	113. a	114. a	115. b	116. b	117. a	118. a	119. a	120. a
121. b	122. a	123. a	124. b	125. a	126. b	127. b	128. a	129. a	130. b
131. b	132. b	133. b	134. a	135. b	136. a	137. b	138. a	139. a	140. a
141. b	142. a	143. a	144. a	145. a	146. b				

Chapter 9

1. b	2. a	3. b	4. a	5. b	6. a	7. a	8. a	9. a	10. b
11. a	12. a	13. b	14. a	15. b	16. b	17. b	18. a	19. b	20. a
21. a	22. b	23. b	24. b	25. b	26. b	27. b	28. a	29. a	30. a
31. b	32. b	33. b	34. b	35. a	36. a	37. b	38. a	39. b	40. a
41. b	42. b	43. b	44. b	45. a	46. b	47. b	48. a	49. a	50. a
51. a	52. a	53. a	54. b	55. b	56. b	57. b	58. b	59. b	60. a
61. b	62. b	63. b	64. a	65. a	66. a	67. b	68. b	69. b	70. b
71. b	72. b	73. a	74. b	75. b	76. a	77. a	78. b	79. b	80. a
81. b	82. a	83. b	84. a	85. a	86. a	87. a	88. a	89. a	90. a
91. b	92. a	93. b	94. a	95. b	96. a	97. b	98. a	99. b	100. b
101. a	102. b	103. a	104. b	105. b	106. b	107. a	108. a	109. b	110. b
111. a	112. a	113. a	114. b	115. a	116. a	117. a	118. a	119. b	120. b
121. a	122. b	123. b	124. b	125. b	126. b	127. b	128. b	129. a	130. b
131. a	132. a	133. a	134. b	135. a	136. a	137. a	138. a	139. b	140. b
141. a	142. b	143. a	144. b						

Chapter 10

1. a	2. a	3. b	4. b	5. b	6. b	7. a	8. a	9. a	10. a
11. b	12. b	13. a	14. a	15. b	16. a	17. b	18. a	19. a	20. a
21. b	22. b	23. a	24. b	25. a	26. b	27. b	28. a	29. a	30. b
31. a	32. b	33. b	34. b	35. a	36. b	37. a	38. a	39. a	40. b
41. a	42. b	43. b	44. a	45. b					

Chapter 11

1. b	2. a	3. a	4. a	5. a	6. a	7. a	8. a	9. a	10. b
11. b	12. b	13. a	14. b	15. b	16. b	17. b	18. b	19. a	20. a
21. b	22. a	23. b	24. b	25. a	26. a	27. b	28. b	29. a	30. a
31. a	32. b	33. a	34. b	35. a	36. b	37. a	38. a	39. a	40. b
41. a									